Born in 1958, Fintan O'Toole
politics and current affairs. A col
presenter on BBC 2's **The Late S**
Award for Supreme Contributio
include two volumes of essays, *Black Hole, Green Card* and *A Mass for Jesse James*, a study of the playwright Tom Murphy, *The Politics of Magic*, and his examination of the Irish Beef Tribunal, *Meanwhile Back at the Ranch*, which was a No 1 bestseller in Ireland.

By the same author

A Mass for Jesse James
— A Journey Through 1980s Ireland

Black Hole, Green Card
— The Disappearance of Ireland

Tom Murphy: The Politics of Magic
— The Work and Times of Tom Murphy

All available from New Island Books.

A Radical Guide to

MACBETH
& HAMLET

For Leaving Cert
and University Students

Fintan O'Toole

NEW
ISLAND
BOOKS

Dublin

Macbeth & Hamlet
is published in 1995 by
New Island Books
2, Brookside,
Dundrum Road,
Dublin 14,
Ireland

ISBN 1 874597 19 7

New Island Books receives financial assistance from
The Arts Council (An Comharile Ealaíon)
Dublin, Ireland

Macbeth & Hamlet is a revised and abridged version of the
author's *No More Heroes*, published by Raven Arts Press, 1990.

Cover Design by Jon Berkeley,
Typesetting by Graphic Resources,
Printed in Ireland by Colour Books, Ltd.

Contents

For Clare with love

1

Shakespeare is Hard, but So is Life

1.   Why is Shakespeare so boring?

The plays of William Shakespeare were written on the playing fields
of Eton. Or rather, the plays of Shakespeare as they tend to be taught
in school, were. Very often, *Hamlet* or *Macbeth*, *King Lear* or
Othello are made to seem as if they have very little to do with the
theatre, with the seventeenth century, with a man trying to create
new rituals for a world that was changing at a frightening pace, and
everything to do with building character, with the nineteenth
century, with teaching us lessons about how we should behave.
They are the mental equivalent of a cold shower, shocking, awful,
but in some obscure way good for you, bracing you for the terrors
of life and keeping your mind off bad thoughts about politics,
society and the way the world changes. They are an ordeal after
which you're supposed to feel better, a kind of mental muesli that
cleans out the system and purges the soul. And, like muesli, they are
boring, fruity and full of indigestible roughage.

   The plays that Shakespeare actually wrote, on the other hand, are
full of great stories, extraordinary people, wonderfully rich
language and a skill with drama that has seldom been matched. They
are not always easy, partly because the language of the sixteenth and
seventeenth centuries, even when it appears to be the same as ours,
can work very differently. When, for instance, Henry Vaughan in
the seventeenth century writes "How fair a prospect is a bright
backside", he doesn't mean what you think he might mean; he's
saying that it is nice to have a garden behind your house. And it
works the other way too - Hamlet can sound like he's talking very
respectably when in fact what he's saying is pure filth. So

Shakespeare's language takes a bit of work. Shakespeare is hard, but so is life, and so long as you can see that there's a lot of life in Shakespeare, then the effort begins to make sense.

What doesn't make any sense is the idea that Shakespeare is trying to demonstrate moral ideas to us, that he's a kind of excruciatingly long-winded head nun. If you look at him this way, then he's not just boring and banal, he's also pretty stupid. One set of school notes on *Macbeth*, for instance, tells us that in "moralistic terms, the Tragic hero and in particular Macbeth, may be seen as a warning to all that evil will be punished in this life as well as the next." Leaving aside the fact that this is not a particularly startling thing to want to tell us, and that Shakespeare might have been better employed writing sermons rather than plays if this was really what he wanted to do, we might well ask what moral message Shakespeare was trying to give us. The message of *Macbeth* is that it's a bad idea to kill kings. The message of *Hamlet* is that Hamlet should have killed the King sooner. Othello is doomed because he is too jealous of what he has. Lear is doomed because he is not jealous enough and wants to give away what he has. If this is what Shakespeare is about, then he's clearly not very good at it. Either there is something else entirely going on in his plays, or else we should all go back to watching soap operas where at least the moral messages are fairly consistent.

2.   What about the Tragic Flaw?

Before we can begin to understand, and therefore enjoy, Shakespeare's tragedies, there is a great deal of undergrowth to be cleared away, all that stuff about Tragic Heroes, Tragic Flaws, Fear and Pity, Character, and so on. Almost every school textbook on one of Shakespeare's tragedies starts out by showing that there is a thing called Tragedy which was defined by a man called Aristotle two thousand years ago and that the play in question, *Hamlet*, *King Lear*, or whatever, conforms to this definition. The assumption seems to be that if for some reason the play did not do what Aristotle said a tragedy should do, then it would somehow cease to be any good and we wouldn't want to read it or see it. By a happy coincidence the textbooks always find that there is no difficulty in showing that

Shakespeare's plays were in fact written to Aristotle's formula, that they are therefore the Real Thing, and that it's okay to go ahead and study them.

The reason *Hamlet* or *Macbeth* have to get a dog licence signed by a Greek who died hundreds of years before the birth of Christ has very little to do with ancient Greece and still less to do with Elizabethan England. But it does have a lot to do with Victorian Britain, with the critics and teachers of nineteenth-century England who laid down many of the categories through which we are still looking at Shakespeare. Shakespeare himself may or may not have been aware of Aristotle's book, *The Poetics*, from which the rules of what tragedy is supposed to be like are derived. We know very little about Shakespeare's life and very little about what he read other than what he used for his plays, but even if he was familiar with Aristotle's "rules", he felt free to ignore them.

The strongest of the so-called Aristotelian rules was the idea of the unities of time, place and action - the idea that tragedies should happen in a single day, in a single place and through a single story. Shakespeare's plays can take up to sixteen years to unfold, hop all over the place, and usually include at least two connected stories. They show no interest whatsoever in the classical rules of tragedy as Aristotle was supposed to have written them. And anyway, Aristotle was merely trying to describe what he thought the best writers of tragedy in his own time were doing.

The only evidence of Shakespeare's attitude to Aristotle that we have from his plays is that he didn't know very much about him. Aristotle is mentioned twice in Shakespeare: once as having written before Homer (which he didn't), and once as being the opposite to Ovid, references that are either wrong or simply obscure. The most important of Aristotle's ideas about tragedy, "catharsis" (the idea that tragedy works by purging our emotions), is never mentioned by Shakespeare and is mentioned only once by any Elizabethan writer: and then only to mock at it.

Even the word "tragedy" itself is something that is forced onto Shakespeare's plays long after they were written. The Stationers' Register, which recorded the titles of his plays in Shakespeare's own time, lists *Hamlet* as a "revenge", *King Lear* as a "history", *Antony and Cleopatra* as "a book called Antony and Cleopatra". *Othello* is listed as a tragedy, but then so are *Richard II* and *Richard III*, which we now call "history plays".

When the plays were printed during Shakespeare's lifetime, their categorisation as tragedies is even more dubious. *Hamlet* is a "tragical history", *King Lear* is a "true chronicle history". Whatever else he was doing, Shakespeare was not sitting down to write something which was called "tragedy" and which followed prescribed rules. He certainly knew that he was *not* writing the most respected and highbrow kind of tragedy of his day, the one which followed classical (mostly Roman) models.

3.   So how did Greek ideas of tragedy get attached to Shakespeare?

The habit of seeing Shakespeare through Aristotle comes from Victorian England. The Victorians were at the centre of a great world Empire and liked to think of themselves as the essence of modern civilisation. Since they thought of ancient Greece as the essence of classical civilisation, they naturally wanted to identify themselves with it as much as possible. If they could show that Shakespeare, a central part of their own culture, was really the first cousin once removed of their beloved Aristotle, then Aristotle's ideas about tragedy would clean up Shakespeare, make him once and for all respectable, fit him in with their own taste for moral seriousness and good example. Out of this combination of Aristotle and soup-soap-and-salvation morality came the idea of the Tragic Flaw.

Victorian thinking about Shakespeare, much of which we have inherited, was dominated by Matthew Arnold's idea that literature had to be thought of as offering help to people who were perplexed about how to live. Living in what they considered to be a very stable and ordered society, the Victorians weren't much interested in those aspects of Shakespeare (easily the most important ones) which are about social and political change, about instability and its consequences. On the whole, they tended to view public affairs in general with distaste, as something which made life crude and corrupted its finer values. What interested them were the peculiarities of Shakespeare's characters and the possibility which they offered for some kind of moral guidance. They also tended to regard the stories of Shakespeare's plays as outlandish and far-fetched, as a crude concession to the populace, saved only by the genius of Shakespeare's poetry. So they split his characters from his stories and gave us the notion of looking at Shakespeare's characters in isolation from his plots, from what is happening to them and around them. The main problem with this is that it makes much of what happens in Shakespeare almost incomprehensible and almost all of it very boring.

As well as reflecting their own view of the world, this idea of what Shakespeare was about also reflected the Victorian theatre. Victorian theatre was dominated by great actor-managers and by the picture-frame stage. Both of these contributed to the idea of the star as the really important thing in the play, so for instance, *Hamlet* was about the actor playing Hamlet, to a lesser extent the actor playing Ophelia, and a few hangers-on to make up the numbers. Sir Walter Scott, for instance, wrote at this time that it was no longer the poetry or the plot which drew an audience to *Hamlet* but the desire to compare some turn of gesture or intonation in Kemble's performance with that of Garrick. This gave a great impetus to the isolated study of the Tragic Hero and of isolated moments in the tragedies, the big scenes and particularly the soliloquies which were the testing-ground of great heroic acting. Good modern productions of Shakespeare have long since moved on from this way of playing Shakespeare and towards the idea that, as the director Peter Brook has put it, "Each moment in Shakespeare should be as important as every other; each speaker should be the 'lead' as he speaks." But the way that Shakespeare is taught is still stuck with the actor-managers of the Victorian stage.

4.   What did we get from the Victorians?

There are three basic ideas which we have taken from the Victorians via Aristotle and which combine to make the study of Shakespeare so tedious:

i. The Idea of the Tragic Flaw, which invites us to ask the question what is wrong with these people? and to come up with witheringly useless answers - Macbeth's flaw is ambition, Hamlet's is indecision. One set of notes widely used in schools, tells us that the Tragic Hero should be "someone whose misfortunes are brought upon him by some error of judgement on his part. This error of judgement may arise from a flaw in his character, some human weakness. It is essential that to some extent he contributes to his own downfall. A simple "rule of thumb" definition of a Tragic Hero that should be adequate for general purposes might be that he is a potentially noble person who, through some flaw in his character, helps to bring about his own downfall, and who, by suffering, acquires self-knowledge, and so purges his faults."

The problem with this notion, which is taken directly from Aristotle without any reference to the enormous differences between Greek tragic heroes and Shakespearian ones is that Shakespeare's plays make no consistent sense when seen in this way. It is also that many of those protagonists can only appear as less than intelligent. If you look at Othello from the point of view that he is merely jealous then it is clear that Othello must not be very intelligent. And if he's not very intelligent, then he's not very interesting. If Macbeth's ambition is merely a flaw in his character, then he's just another psychopath with an eye for the main chance. If Hamlet's indecision is a flaw in his character then he's wasting our time and his own and we are all supposed to believe that killing your uncle is a good thing. If Lear is merely a vain old man, then why does Gloucester have to have his eyes put out? And there is not the slightest evidence that any of Shakespeare's tragic protagonists understand themselves better at the end of the play than at the beginning. They may understand their world better, but that is a very different thing.

The whole idea of the Tragic Flaw presupposes that there is a kind of justice working in Shakespeare's tragedies, that even if the sufferings of the Hero, like those of King Lear, are out of all proportion to his supposed flaw, nevertheless the tragedies are about people bringing destruction on themselves. But this is exactly the opposite of what happens in the plays. The tragedies are littered with innocent corpses, people who have done nothing to bring death on themselves but who nevertheless meet it, often in the most violent and shocking way. Shakespeare goes out of his way in the tragedies to give us meaningless, gratuitous deaths. If ambition is Macbeth's flaw, what is Lady Macduff's? If indecision is Hamlet's flaw, what is Ophelia's? The whole idea of the Tragic Flaw can be maintained only by searching out some evil in Lady Macduff or Ophelia (as some critics have ludicrously tried to do, ending up with complete nonsense) or by completely separating the Heroes from the plays in which we find them, by pretending that Shakespeare wrote his Heroes according to one set of rules and everyone else in the plays according to another. Again, Shakespeare comes out looking confused, inconsistent and hardly worth studying.

The real function of the Tragic Flaw theory is to reduce Shakespeare's tragedies, to pretend that they are neat moral fables which we can easily assimilate. It tames the plays and makes them comfortable, bringing them back to a rational little world in which they offer no challenge to our way of looking at things.

ii. The Idea of the Tragic Hero, which cuts the central character off from the play and then goes on to examine in isolation the characters of all of the other people who affect what happens to him. In Shakespeare, as in all good drama, it is not character that is interesting, but the interplay between characters - the action. If you isolate the individuals in a play and then try to analyse their characters in a static way, they are not only tedious but impossible to understand. The writer C.S. Lewis, who had the experience of marking school exams put it well, with reference to Chauntecleer and Pertelote, a cock and a hen in a poem by Chaucer: "I once had a whole batch of School Certificate answers on the "Nuns's Priests' Tale" by boys whose form-master was apparently a breeder of poultry. Everything that Chaucer had said in describing Chauntecleer and Pertelote was treated by them solely as evidence about the precise breed of these two birds... They proved beyond doubt that Chauntecleer was very different from our modernised specialised strains and much closer to the old English "barn door fowl". But I couldn't help feeling that they had missed something. I believe that our attention to Hamlet's character in the usual sense misses almost as much."

The whole idea of looking at character in this sense in Shakespeare's plays is misplaced. Characterisation in the modern theatrical sense is a word which comes into use in the English language only in the mid-nineteenth century. Character, in the sense of a part assumed by an actor, comes in a hundred years earlier, but still a very long time after Shakespeare's death. To talk about

Shakespeare's characters in isolation from the action, to discuss their psychology and motivation, is to treat Shakespearian tragedies as if they were nineteenth century naturalistic plays. It is to miss their uniqueness and their power. It is also, all too often, to build up a set of stereotypes which take the place of the complex and often deliberately contradictory people that Shakespeare gives us.

The idea that there is a set of characters lodged in each Shakespearian play which only needs to be satisfactorily defined in order for us to understand the play, is one which ignores the whole nature of Shakespearian tragedy as theatre. Theatre is historical - the perception of individual theatrical characters changes over time. In the nineteenth century, for instance, Charles Lamb thought it was impossible to actually put King Lear on the stage, because "To see Lear acted is to see an old man tottering about the stage with a walking stick." Nowadays, no one would dream of a Lear who is either tottering or with a walking stick. European poets of the nineteenth century invented a Hamlet who was very like themselves - romantic, enervated, sick at heart. Nowadays we may see Hamlet in our own mould, as a twentieth- century cynic. In the case of Othello, far from agreeing as to the nature of his character, critics and actors have been unable to even to agree on the colour of his skin. It may seem perfectly obvious to us that *Othello* is a story which depends absolutely on the relationship between a black man and a white woman, but to the more openly racist nineteenth century, even this most obvious aspect of Othello's character could, indeed must, be overlooked. A. C. Bradley, the Victorian critic from whom many of our ideas about Shakespeare's tragedies come, recognised that Shakespeare had intended Othello to be black, but still thought that this would be more than a modern audience could be expected to stomach: "Perhaps if we saw Othello coal-black with the bodily eye, the aversion of our blood, an aversion which comes as near to being merely physical as anything human can, would overpower our imagination..." Because Bradley and his British contemporaries were racist, Othello could not be black, whatever Shakespeare's views on the matter. And Macbeth, whom nineteenth century critics saw as fierce and primitive, can be envisaged in our time by an American middle-class writer like Mary McCarthy almost as an American middle-class businessman: "A commonplace man who talks in commonplaces, a golfer, one might guess."

What these examples suggest is that it is the way we interpret the play that shapes our understanding of the characters and not the other way round. We decide what it is that the play has to say to us in our own time and then we shape the characters accordingly. And even then we are interested in the characters, not in their character. We want to know how they respond, how they shape and are shaped by all the things and people they encounter. Hamlet's character is only of interest to us if we ever have to write him a job reference. Only if we stick to the idea of the Tragic Flaw, which is a kind of secular version of Original Sin, seeing the people of the plays as ready-assembled packages complete with built-in flaw, does the idea of a fixed character make any sense at all.

But the whole point about creations like Hamlet and Macbeth is that they have no fixed centre, that they are all responses, never quite the same person from one moment to the next, changing even in the course of a single speech perhaps two or three times. At the end of the plays we do not know much more about their character than at the start - what we feel is that we have experienced something extraordinary through them and with them. Shakespeare's tragic protagonists remain enigmatic right to the end. If they didn't we would lose interest in them. They are interesting precisely because they have no fixed characters.

If we try to analyse character in isolation from the dramatic action, what we end up with is scenes which don't make sense. There are many scenes in the tragedies which are about giving us information, in which the people who are speaking are not revealing their characters but telling us what is going on. There are very many others which, as we will see in discussing the individual plays, are impossible to understand if we see them as being about developing the individual characters. And we must also remember that very often the people who talk most about themselves, who give us most material for character analysis, people like Hamlet, are the very ones who remain enigmatic, whose motives and aims remain most mysterious. We also have to remember that isolating characters from their situation makes for a grossly misleading interpretation of what other characters are like.

One of the reasons why Shakespeare's characters fossilise into stereotypes is that we tend to believe what other characters say about them, without taking into account the dramatic situation, the fact that they may have good reasons to tell lies. Someone like Claudius in *Hamlet*, for instance, gets characterised as a filthy lascivious monster. We don't actually see him being filthy and lascivious, and we know that Hamlet has his own reasons for describing Claudius in this way, but the hunt for a fixed character for Claudius makes it useful to take Hamlet's assessment on face value. What gets overlooked is the fact that the crude language which Hamlet uses when he's talking about Claudius may tell us more about Hamlet than it does about Claudius.

iii. The Whole Idea of the Soliloquy, the notion that Shakespeare's heroes spend a great deal of time talking to themselves and, in a kind of spiritual striptease, revealing their true selves to us. It has become fundamental to the teaching of Shakespeare that the soliloquies are the most important part of any tragedy, that they deserve to be isolated, directed and analysed as the real key to the character of the Tragic Hero. Most guides to Shakespeare will tell you that in soliloquy lies truth. Nothing is more calculated to make Shakespeare's protagonists seem foolish and incomprehensible than the idea that they spend a lot of their days gazing at their navels and talking to themselves. In the plays that Shakespeare wrote, they don't.

Again our idea of the soliloquies is one which comes, not from the seventeenth century but from the nineteenth, in particular from the Romantic movement. The Romantics were interested above all in subjective feeling, in the idea of self-expression. They found, or thought they found, in Shakespeare's soliloquies a subjective form of drama, a kind of theatre that was about self-revelation. The whole centre of interest in Shakespeare's plays came to be located in the soliloquies. Shakespeare's True Confessions were born. And as the nineteenth century went on, the changes that took place in theatrical conventions made the soliloquies look more and more like people talking to themselves. And the whole interest in the centrality of the soliloquies as absolutely truthful self-revelation went hand-in-hand with the increasingly psychological notion of character. The soliloquies were important because in them the heroes were revealing their own characters for us.

The problem with all of this is that it has almost nothing to do with the kind of theatre which Shakespeare created and that it blinds us to many of the things that are going on in the plays. It again misses the point that the tragedies are first and foremost plays. In the theatre, it is possible for an actor on stage to speak **by** himself, but it is not possible for an actor on stage to speak **to** himself. Unless the actors are really lousy, there is always an audience, always someone listening and watching. The difficulty arises with the fact that since the nineteenth century it has been the general convention of theatre that the actors pretend not to notice the audience, and that when they are talking they are talking only to each other. When there is only actor on the stage, he must be talking to himself. This is a convention which works for a great deal of modern drama.

It has, however, nothing whatsoever to do with Shakespeare. In Shakespeare's theatre there is no convention which says that an actor cannot notice and address the audience. There is therefore no reason to believe that when an actor is talking alone on stage he is not talking to the audience, that instead of a pure stream of internal monologue the actor is not indirectly addressing the audience. The soliloquies are not, therefore, in any real sense private and internal. They are a form of speech which is somewhere between the private and the public, which tries to marry the concerns of the individual with those of the collective. In the concern with the soliloquies as a pure form of self-expression, it is forgotten that even some of the most intimate soliloquies in *Hamlet* or *Macbeth* use the word "we" rather than the word "I". As a consequence, many of these speeches are almost completely misunderstood.

The way in which this works in *Macbeth* and *Hamlet* will be discussed in the subsequent chapters on those plays, but the important point here is that there is not, in Shakespeare's tragedies, a mere switch between public speech and private speech. There are in fact whole layers of different kinds of speech, ranging from highly formal public exchange to intimate formal conversation to private informal exchange to different kinds of monologues. By simply focussing in on the idea of the soliloquy as the truest form of speech in these plays, you lose the whole drama of the way in which Shakespeare moves all the time from one kind of speech to another, blurring the borders between the private and the public. By not paying attention to the question of who is talking to whom and, more importantly, who is listening in, a great deal of the drama of the plays is lost. First and foremost the soliloquies and all other speeches in Shakespeare are not poems which can be taken out and studied, they are pieces of dramatic action.

5.   So what is Tragedy?

Shakespeare, as we have seen, chose to ignore the Aristotelian rules for tragedy, and it is therefore absurd to analyse Shakespeare's tragedies as if they were versions of the Greek model. It's not that Shakespeare was unaware of what the rules were, it is that he positively decided that a different kind of theatre was needed if he was to successfully dramatise his own society. The most famous work of literary criticism of Elizabethan England was Sir Philip Sidney's *Defence of Poesie*. In it Sidney laid down the Aristotelian rules: "The stage should always represent but one place, and the uttermost time presupposed in it should be, both by Aristotle's precept and common reason, but one day. Moreover tragedy and comedy must be kept severely apart and the playwright should not thrust in the clown by head and shoulders to play a part in majestical matters." Shakespeare, of course broke all of these rules and knew he was breaking them. He didn't break them because he wasn't up to writing classical plays on the Greek and Roman lines. He could do it if he wanted to: *The Comedy of Errors* uses a single place and a single day. *Julius Caesar* is a perfect classical tragedy. He broke them because they were not good enough to deal with the complexities of the world he was living in. *Hamlet* and *Macbeth* are tragedies but tragedies of a kind which cannot be analysed in terms of Tragic Flaws and Tragic Heroes. To understand what kind of tragedies they are, we have to understand what kind of world they were intended to reflect.

Successful tragedy is not something which is particularly common in the long history of the theatre. It gets written only at certain times, times when there is a great deal of tension between two sets of values, two world views, two ways of thinking about how individuals relate to their societies. The tragic figures are those who get caught in the middle between these two world views, and who therefore literally can do nothing right. They can do nothing right because what is right in one world is not right in another. They act according to one set of values in a world which is still dominated by a different set of values. Clear distinctions, the borders between things that are supposed to be opposite, are breaking down. The interesting and dramatic thing about people in a tragedy is that they are caught on those borders.

6. What was England like in Shakespeare's time?

For one thing it was highly stratified and the division between rich and poor was overwhelmingly obvious. On the one hand, between a third of the population lived at subsistence level and was chronically underemployed. On the other hand, at the top, there was the traditional landed elite, now challenged for power by the rising professional groups: merchants, lawyers, clergymen and administrative officials. The landowners and professional classes, though only five per cent of the population, between them enjoyed a larger proportion of the national income than did all the lower classes (over fifty per cent of the population) put together.

The social elite of Shakespeare's time was highly educated, and shortly after Shakespeare's death it was estimated that about two and half per cent of the young male population was receiving some form of third level education, a proportion that would not be attained again in England until well into the twentieth century. But at the same time between half and two-thirds of the adult population was unable to read. This was no simple, unified, primitive world, therefore, but a highly divided and diverse society, where social and intellectual change had long been at work, moving in many different directions.

It is a world which has been described this way by Grigori Kozintsev: "Everything was shuffled - the groan of death with the cry of birth. The lash whistled in medieval torture chambers, but the click of abacus balls was heard all the louder. Feudal outlaws discussed the price of wool, and rumours about the success of Flemish textiles were intermingled with authentic details of the witches' Sabbath."

So what should be the most obvious thing about Shakespeare's time is that it is a period of rapid change, of the transition between one world view and another. This obvious fact was obscured by the nineteenth century critics who wanted to look back on Elizabethan England as a Golden Age, a time of order, stability and a fixed universe, and to view Shakespeare in this light. This is where the notion of Shakespeare as timeless, as the bearer of universal values, comes from. But in fact Shakespeare's time is anything but stable, and his tragedies are plays which dramatise traumatic change and the way it affects our whole way of looking at the world.

It was certainly obvious to Shakespeare's contemporaries that they were living through a period of crisis. Five years before Shakespeare's death, the poet John Donne wrote that:

'Tis all in pieces, all coherence gone;
All just supply and all relation:
Prince, subject, father, son, are things forgot,
For every man alone that he hath got
To be a Phoenix and that then can be
None of that kind of which he is but he.

(The First Anniversary)

Looking at his and Shakespeare's England, Donne saw a world in which all order and coherence had fallen apart, in which the hierarchy of relations both within the state and within the family was breaking down, in which men were getting the idea that they were uniquely their own invention rather than the product of their place and status within a highly stratified society. His poem could also have been an exact description of Shakespeare's tragedies, of the inter-related breakdown of family and state in each of them, of the Phoenix-like Hamlet and Macbeth, each believing that he is a self-made man, that he owes his individuality not to his status but to his free will. Their tragedy is that their world is not yet quite like that, that the pull of order and hierarchy is still very strong, not least within their own minds. The tragedies are about the conflict between status on the one hand and individual power on the other and what dooms Macbeth and Hamlet is that for none of them do status and power go together at the same time.

Shakespeare's age is the age in which a whole new class, the capitalist and professional middle-class comes to substantial power and prominence in England. Elizabethan England depended on foreign trade and foreign trade led to the rise of merchant capital. The making of large amounts of money by a new class of people who were neither the traditional land-owning elite nor the mass of peasants and labourers meant that Shakespeare's lifetime became the period of the most rapid advance in mining and manufacture that England was to know until the Industrial Revolution of the late eighteenth century. And at the same time, the centralisation of state power and the beginnings of a foreign trading empire made the development of a large professional, educated, administrative class necessary. These in turn brought the new humanist Renaissance ideas into vogue in England. Both economically and intellectually, therefore, the absolutely fixed hierarchy of the old feudal order was being challenged as never before. There are two value systems, two world views in competition, and this is the essential context in which to understand Shakespeare's tragedies.

The extent of the changes which were underway in Shakespeare's times cannot be overstated. James I, who was on the throne when all of the major tragedies except *Hamlet* were written, preached that kings ruled by Divine Right and many political writers argued that the property of every subject should be completely at the disposal of the king. Within thirty-five years of Shakespeare's death, the English had executed their king and politics was being conducted as a rational inquiry, a matter of utility, experience, common sense. James I wrote a treatise on witches, and was no more superstitious than most of his subjects, who still took alchemy and astrology very seriously indeed. By the second half of the seventeenth century, science was in the ascendent and fairies, witches, astrology and alchemy were no longer respectable beliefs for an educated man to hold. In Shakespeare's time, the earth was the centre of a universe in which God and the Devil continuously intervened. In the second half of the century in which the tragedies were written, Newton would show the universe to be a self-moving machine. A world in which everything, both natural and supernatural, had its proper place and category, was giving way to one in which both society and the universe seemed to be made up of competing atoms. Shakespeare's tragedies are written at a time when nothing less than a fundamental re-ordering of our understanding of the world, the categories by which we make sense of our experience, is in progress. The plays contain and dramatise that re-ordering and to fail to understand this is to fail to understand the plays.

7.   So Shakespeare is part of the Renaissance?

Shakespeare can properly be described as part of the English Renaissance, but only if the Renaissance is understood in certain ways. We think of the Renaissance as the time in which European culture re-possessed the cultural artefacts of the classical Greek and Roman civilisation, and because Shakespeare is a Renaissance figure this encourages the tendency to think of him in terms of that classical world, in particular in terms of Aristotle and Greek tragedy. But this is to misunderstand both Shakespeare and the Renaissance. The repossession of Greek and Roman antiquity is not so much a statement of continuity, of the continuance of classical into modern Europe. It is the opposite, for to repossess something implies a recognition of precisely how different it is from your own culture. The success of the Renaissance presupposed the recognition of a fundamental discontinuity between the culture of the present and that of the distant past. It implies that you have started to think of your own culture, not as absolute, which was the feudal conception of the Middle Ages, but as relative, as something to which there are fundamentally different alternatives. Shakespeare is a Renaissance writer only in the sense that he is aware of the extent to which nothing is absolute. In the tragedies there is an overwhelming sense that all of the most fundamental values of society have ceased to be absolute and have become relative.

8.   But surely, the fate of Shakespeare's heroes is inevitable. That means that a lot of things in Shakespeare's world are still predictable?

This raises another of the hoary cliches about schoolbook Shakespeare. It is an article of faith, again taken from Aristotle, that in Shakespearian tragedy the downfall of the hero must seem inevitable. One set of notes on *King Lear*, for instance, tells us at the outset that "In tragedy, the hero's fall is inevitable, and presented as being so. The tragic dramatist organises his world in such a way that the chances of a happy outcome are nil." This is largely true of Greek drama where in general a train of action has been set in motion long before the play even opens and cannot be undone. There is a cold logic working itself out and we can only sit and watch as it reaches towards its inevitable conclusion. But this is almost completely untrue of Shakespeare. In Shakespeare there is no cold logic and indeed no logic at all. It is not inevitable that Othello should kill Desdemona, indeed it is amazing that he should do so. It is not inevitable that Cordelia in *King Lear* should be hanged, indeed the whole point of it is that it is gratuitous. It is not inevitable that Hamlet should die, indeed Shakespeare goes out of his way to make his death messy, complicated, fumbled. Far from it being inevitable that Macbeth should be killed, Shakespeare goes to great lengths to make his death a refutation of the idea of inevitability, showing prophecies to us which imply that everything is pre-ordained, but then exposing them as tricks.

The doctrine of inevitability implies an absolute world, a world in which once the stone is dropped in the pool, the ripples will be unstoppable. Shakespeare on the other hand gives us a relative world, a world in which causes don't have their effects, in which almost nothing is predictable, never mind inevitable. A stone is dropped in one pool and the ripples spread in another, seemingly miles away. Shakespeare is not concerned with a logical world but with an irrational one, a world made irrational by the fact that it contains two different sets of values, two separate logics, which refuse to hold their places.

In all four of the major tragedies, the central figure is someone who loses a sense of himself, whose grip on his own identity becomes weaker and weaker, leading to real or feigned madness (in the case of Hamlet and Lear) or to the kind of complete dependence on the words and judgements of others which is the mark of a loss of faith in one's own independent identity (Macbeth with the witches, Othello with Iago). This reflects the fact that in Shakespeare's time there is a transition in the way in which one's identity is defined. In feudal, mediaeval society, your identity is your role, and your role is determined by your birth and position, so long as that birth is legitimate. Legitimate birth confers not just a right of inheritance, but a whole set of duties and prescribed behaviour. If you want to know who you are, you examine your position in society. You are your status.

In the kind of commercial, capitalist world which is emerging in Shakespeare's time, you are your power. Your identity is the sum of your achievements. It is something you make for yourself. You are what you do. The tragedy of Lear and Macbeth, of Hamlet and Othello, is that they think they operate according to both of these principles, that they can base themselves both on a world of status and a world of power, even though these two worlds are contradictory and in active conflict.

It is the fate of these four men to enjoy either status or power, but never both together. Hamlet, as a royal prince who has been denied succession to the throne, has status but not power. Othello, as a mercenary general admired for his skill but disdained for his colour, has power but no status. Lear keeping the title of king but not the reality of the office, has status but no power. Macbeth, killing Duncan, gains power but not status, not that essential aspect of the status of the king, the right to hand on his power to his children and his children's children in an unbroken assertion of order and tradition. Power and status are two worlds, two governing values, the one from the new capitalist world, the other from the old feudal one, which refuse to come together for any of the great tragic figures of Shakespeare's plays. And it is in the failure of this equation, the fact that they are caught between two worlds, that they are lost.

Shakespeare, of course, doesn't present us with abstractions called "power" and "status" in his plays; he gives us people trying to live their lives. And the way in which this conflict is played out is in the relationship between men and women. In each of the four plays, a man becomes separated from a woman. Lear loses Cordelia, Hamlet loses Ophelia, Othello loses Desdemona, Macbeth loses Lady Macbeth. And in each the woman who is lost represents the man's link to an ordered, traditional society. For Lear, it is Cordelia who puts forward the notion of proper degree and proportion in things, of everything having its proper place. Losing her, he loses his connection to that ordered, feudal world. For Hamlet, it is Ophelia who might represent marriage, loyalty, traditional morality. For Othello, adrift in the wild world of war, it is Desdemona who represents due loyalty, respectable society, the established moral order. For Macbeth, it is Lady Macbeth, haunted by the demands of conscience, duty and the proper order of things, who represents the moral universe with which he has broken. With the women representing one set of values and the men another, it is hardly surprising that men and women cannot function together in any kind of wholeness in these plays, that the sexual order as well the social and political order, breaks down.

This is why images of childlessness, of sterility, of the lack of continuity between the generations, are such powerful images in these tragedies. If men and women cannot fit together in harmony, then sterility looms. Hamlet condemns Ophelia to sterility. ("Get thee to a nunnery".) The extent of Lady Macbeth's unnaturalness is measured by the fact that she is prepared to murder the baby at her breast. The farthest reach of her husband's madness is not the murder of his king or of his friend but that of Macduff's little children. When Macduff hears of the event his curse on Macbeth (leading to all sorts of contortions on the part of literal-minded commentators as to whether the Macbeths have children or not) is "He has no children". When Macbeth himself wants to express the ultimate horror he can imagine, it is the killing of the seeds of future generations : "though the treasure of all nature's germens tumble together/Even till destruction sicken." And the very same image appears at the climax of *King Lear*: "Crack nature's molds, all germens spill at once." In Shakespeare's tragedies, things are changing so fast that the whole idea of human continuity seems to be threatened. There is even, in *King Lear*, a powerful sense that the end of the world may be at hand.

9.   **That's all very well, but we have to learn about iambic pentameters and blank verse.**

It is not just the content and the imagery of Shakespeare's tragedies that is shaped by the extremely fluid nature of the world he lives in, it is also the very kind of poetry which he writes. Shakespeare's iambic pentameter is not just a matter of individual style, it is a form of poetic rhythm that is superbly well adapted to including a whole range of contradictory things. It is free and boundless, able to sweep over an extraordinary range of dramatic situations (from the very intimate to the formal and public) and a huge diversity of speaking characters. But at the same time it also retains a strong sense of order, of shape and of form. The whole nature of the poetry embodies the contradictions that Shakespeare is dramatising: the contradiction between order on the one hand and individuality on the other, between feudalism and capitalism. And it is precisely the containing power of this poetry, the extraordinary inclusiveness of it, that gives the tragedies their formal power, their sense that in spite of the fierce tensions which they contain, they are still finished, ordered works of art. The plays invoke chaos without themselves being chaotic.

10. That's the form, but what about the imagery?

The momentous social changes that were taking place in Shakespeare's time help us to understand the kind of conflicts that are going on in his plays. But they don't really tell us all that much about the way the plays work, about how they have their effect on us, about what it is that we feel in watching the plays and why. To understand that we have to ask how the conflicts of Shakespeare's time could be expressed in ways that would seem to have a powerful gut effect on us. And to do that we have to understand something about the nature of tragedy as a social ritual.

All societies, whether they are what we would regard as primitive, tribal societies, or as modern sophisticated ones, have their rituals, and in general these rituals have similar functions. The main function of public rituals is to help us to put an order on our experience, to give us categories through which we can make sense of the multiplicity of the world in which we live. Rituals are basically systems of classification, the simplest ones being organised around simple opposites: left and right, black and white, male and female. They classify things as either one thing or the other, make us comfortable with our experience. And in all societies which have rituals, therefore, things which defy categorisation, which slip between opposites, which refuse to be one thing or the other, are dangerous and powerful.

Shakespeare's tragic protagonists are just such things, and his tragedies are rituals in which those dangerous and powerful things are contained. Shakespeare's tragedies come from a culture in which the whole idea of ritual is very much in question. He writes them at the time of the Protestant reformation, a reformation which presents itself as a deliberate attempt to take the ritual out of religion, to destroy the idea that public religious ceremonies have any ritual or magical function. Significantly, the most radical of the Protestants, the Puritans, saw theatre in the same category as superstitions and rituals, wanting to take the theatricality out of religion and then, after Shakespeare's death, to ban theatre altogether, a step that was absolutely in line with their attitude to religious ceremony.

It's important to realise that for the people of Shakespeare's time and before, religion was not so much a set of beliefs as a set of rituals, and that therefore the loss of those rituals with the rise of

Protestantism left a large gap to be filled. As the historian Keith Thomas has put it, "The church was important...not because of its formalised code of belief but because its rites were an essential accompaniment to the important events in...life - birth, marriage, death...Religion was a ritual method of living, not a set of dogmas." With the changeover to Protestantism, the religious rituals were abandoned, but the things which had given rise to the need for them had not: "the fluctuations of nature, the hazards of fire, the threat of plague and disease, the fear of evil spirits, and all the uncertainties of daily life." And indeed to all of these uncertainties was added the uncertainty of unprecedented economic, political and cultural change. There were needs and no rituals to fill them. The theatre, and in particular Shakespeare, was one way of providing for that need.

In creating his tragedies as secular rituals, Shakespeare shows all categories, all basic opposites, breaking down. In the tragedies the basic opposites by which we are able to make any sense at all of things - life and death, black and white, man and woman - melt into each other. Shakespeare is dealing with a world which is re-ordering its knowledge, with the rise of a class whose first triumphant assault on power 150 years later will be, not the storming of the Bastille, but the writing, by Diderot and D'Alembert, of an Encyclopedia, a new classification of everything that is known. But in Shakespeare's time, that new classification has not yet emerged. The *Summa Theologica* of Saint Thomas Aquinas, which classified all knowledge for the mediaeval world, is no longer good enough, and the Encyclopedia of Diderot and D'Alembert has not yet been written. There is no satisfactory way of categorising experience, so that things refuse to hold their identity and begin to slip into each other, becoming both powerful and dangerous. It is just such things that rituals are there to deal with and it is just things which make up Shakespeare's tragedies.

Things and people which refuse to stay within their proper boundaries both fascinate and horrify us, and as a consequence they take on ritual significance. Monsters like the elephant man and the wolfboy are fascinating because they defy the boundaries of the categories which we use to order our experience. Certain animals make our skin crawl because they slip between categories: slimy reptiles that refuse to belong to either the sea or the land; nasty rodents that come into our houses, yet refuse to conform to the bounds of domestication. In-between animals, those that are neither fish nor flesh, take on special meaning and ritual value. Similarly, toenails or hair, those things which are on the border between ourselves and the material world outside us, go into magic potions. The animals in the witches brew in *Macbeth* - toads, cats, hedge pigs, snakes, newts, frogs, bats, lizards, - are all ambiguous as either reptiles or half-domestic, half-wild. It is not for nothing that the witches chant "Double, double": all of these things have double meanings and are therefore dangerous. Throughout the tragedies, as we shall see in looking at the individual plays, the imagery is of snakes, monsters, humans turning into animals and animals turning into humans, creatures that exist on the dangerous borders between categories. The plays themselves are a kind of witches' brew, where dangerous visions are conjured up in a powerful ritual.

For what is true of animals is even more true of people. Rituals everywhere are very concerned with people who go beyond the normal boundaries, who escape from their proper categories. Tribes have rituals in which a man will leave his band and wander in the forest in the guise of a madman, rituals based on the belief that by leaving the order of society and going out into chaos and disorder some kind of power can be gained. These rituals venture into disorder in a double sense - venturing both beyond the confines of society and into the disordered regions of the mind. Most obviously, this is what happens to King Lear, but in all of the tragedies there are marginal figures, people who are neither one thing nor the other - ghosts, witches, Banquo's unborn heirs, the dead Yorick in *Hamlet* who is momentarily brought back to life.

The protagonists of Shakespeare's tragedies themselves conform to what the anthropologist Mary Douglas has to say about figures who take on ritual significance in tribal societies, who are dangerous and fascinating: "Danger lies in transitional states, simply because transition is neither one state nor the next, it is indefinable." Living in a time of transition, Shakespeare gives us tragic protagonists who are dangerous and powerful, who slip between all of the categories of our experience, and who therefore have about them the fundamental power of ritual. It is not because we can define their characters that Shakespeare's people are interesting to us, but because they are literally indefinable, eluding and denying definition in a deliberate and systematic way. It is not because they teach us lessons that we care about them, but because they enact something that is dangerous, powerful and disturbing.

2

Macbeth: Back to the Future

1. If Shakespeare is so smart, why are there witches in Macbeth?

The witches in *Macbeth* are an embarrassment. Like refugees from an over-enthusiastic Halloween party they wander into this otherwise serious play about power and death and the evils of being too ambitious. They pull ugly faces and mutter mumbo-jumbo about toads and livers. It's not even as if they can be just cut out: not only does the play not make sense without them but, in a way, they are more real than anyone else on stage. We see them first, they define the reality that we are to see, as the play goes on. Not only that, but they know more about what's really going on than anyone else. Actually, and unforgivably, they are closer to the audience's point of view than anyone else in the play: they share their confidences with us, let us know about the little game they are playing with *Macbeth*, function as a kind of audience themselves, maintaining their distance from the action but egging it on to its conclusion.

The best thing to do is to explain them away. They are Shakespeare's way of flattering the new King James, who was fascinated by witches. They are the remnants of a culture that we can no longer understand - terrifying then, laughable now.

But the witches in *Macbeth* are not much like the witches that James was interested in: they slip through definitions rather than being theologically and socially defined as James would have had it. And far from being terrifyingly exotic in the world of *Macbeth*, they are merely examples of the way the whole play behaves. Their slipping through definitions, breaking down categories, refusing to let basic oppositions like male and female, losing and winning, fair and foul, truth and lies remain opposites, is merely the most extreme form of the way the play as a whole works.

The witches are not an aberration, or a sideline. *Macbeth*, unlike *Hamlet* or *King Lear*, doesn't have subplots or digressions. It is, at a mere 2086 lines, remarkable for its compactness, its economy, the speed with which it moves. It is by far the shortest of the tragedies of Shakespeare, so short that there is speculation that the version of *Macbeth* which we have may be itself an abridged one, shortened for performance at court. Either way, *Macbeth* is tightly written: the prominence that the witches have in it is strengthened by the shortness of the play as a whole. Shakespeare meant them to be as important in the overall structure as they still, inescapably, are. Some lines (3, 5 and parts of 4, 1) of the witches are probably not by Shakespeare, but they are irrelevant ones. The witches, on the whole, are almost as central to the play as Macbeth himself.

2.   What do the witches do?

From the start, the function of the witches is to confuse - us and Macbeth. They are the first thing on stage and it is hard to say even what we see when we look at them. Are they natural or supernatural? If they are natural, are they female or male? We usually think of them as female because they are called the Weird Sisters: but it is by no means clear. The actors Shakespeare's own audience would have seen were men or possibly boys - women were not allowed to act on stage. The text tells us, that they are also bearded. Banquo cannot decide: "You should be women/ And yet your beards forbid me to interpret/That you are so." (1, 3, 45-7). And if they are not natural - again Banquo is unsure: They "look not like the inhabitants o' th' earth/And yet are on't. (1, 3, 41-2) - are they real or just a delusion, a projection of some inner fantasy that Macbeth and Banquo have shared?

Theatrically, they are real enough - they are physically present on stage - but, we can never be certain of the degree to which they are projecting the thoughts of those whom they encounter. The first thing Macbeth says in the play, for instance, - "So foul and fair a day I have not seen." (1, 3, 38) - is a direct echo of the witches -

"Fair is foul and foul is fair" (1, 1, 11) - almost, for a moment as if this man whom we haven't seen before were just himself another of the witches. All of these things are consciously and deliberately left uncertain by Shakespeare, making the witches a running, living image, of the loss of definition that is at the heart of the play.

3.   What is it that makes things so unstable, makes things turn into their opposites like this?

For Shakespeare it is money. In another Shakespeare tragedy *Timon of Athens*, written around the same time as *Macbeth*, Timon talks of:

> *Gold? Yellow, glittering, precious gold?..*
> *Thus much of this will make black white, foul fair,*
> *Wrong right, base noble, old young, coward valiant...*
> *This yellow slave*
> *Will knit and break religions, bless th' accursed,*
> *Make the hoar leprosy ador'd, place thieves*
> *And give them title, knee and approbation,*
> *With senators on the bench...(4, 3, 26 -)*

It is money that makes foul fair and one of the earliest images in *Macbeth*, used twice in prominent places in the first three scenes, is of fair becoming foul and foul fair. Opposites are becoming interchangeable, categories are falling apart under the pressure of the rise of new money. One world view is slowly giving way to another, so that two overlapping worlds seem to exist at the same time, the world of order and duty on the one hand and the self-made world of men like Macbeth on the other. It is a frightening transition, one that desperately needs a ritual in which the blurred edges of the categories by which men and women understand their lives can be explored. *Macbeth* is such a ritual, full of things and images that operate not naturalistically, not as a slice of real life, but ritualistically, as a way of calling up and exorcising this slippery, dangerous state.

4.   What is wrong with Macbeth?

Macbeth is a play that literally cannot be understood if it is approached with traditional tools like the analysis of character and the Tragic Flaw. Macbeth's flaw is the easiest of all to name. It is ambition: he tells us so himself. The problem is that when you look at the piece of the play where he talks about his ambition as dramatic action rather than as material for a report on his moral or psychological welfare, it is not so simple. In Act 1, scene 7, Macbeth names the compulsion he feels as "ambition" but as soon as he gives it that name he rejects it. It is precisely when he calls himself ambitious that he is best able to decide not to kill Duncan ("We will proceed no farther in this business.") He talks of ambition, not as a positive reason for action, but as something that is not sufficient to make him act:

I have no spur to prick the sides of my intent, but
only vaulting ambition, which o'erleaps itself and
falls on t'other -
Enter Lady Macbeth. (1, 7, 25 -)

Two things are to be noted about this speech. One is that it is left unfinished, cut off and rendered meaningless by the action. Lady Macbeth comes in and what follows are four lines, each of which ends with a question mark. The giving of a name to the thing that drives Macbeth is immediately undermined by a sequence of inconclusion and uncertainty. The second is that Macbeth's metaphor of mounting and spurring horses is actually hopelessly confused. The metaphor of spurring - done when you are already on your horse - comes before the metaphor of mounting the horse. In other words the effect comes before the cause. To look to this speech which turns cause and effect on their heads for the cause of Macbeth's actions, the root of his character, is to look in the wrong place. Far from giving us the primary cause of what happens, the whole effect of the speech is to make a nonsense of cause and effect altogether.

5.   Where did Shakespeare get the story from?

If you look at what Shakespeare does with his sources for the story of *Macbeth*, the folly of looking for a simple motive for what Macbeth does in the play becomes obvious. He uses two different stories from Holinshed's Chronicles, that of the mild and incompetent King Duncan killed by Macbeth and Banquo, and that of the murder of King Duff by Donwald egged on by his wife. Now both of these killings have clear motives. In the first, Duncan is not particularly up to the job and Macbeth is in league with Banquo, making for a political coup d'etat. In the second, Donwald kills King Duff as an act of revenge, part of a continuing blood-feud. But, although he follows the stories closely in other respects, Shakespeare is at pains to make sure that none of these motives remains in his version of the story: Duncan's stature is enhanced, his kindness to Macbeth emphasised. Banquo is set apart from the murder. Shakespeare, in fact goes to a lot of trouble to make the murder motiveless, to stop us from looking for a straightforward personal motivation on Macbeth's part. The play is about many things, but it is not about Macbeth's character and motives.

If it were, it wouldn't be very interesting. Viewed in isolation as a character, Macbeth is, at the most critical point of the play, merely a tool of his wife's. The murder of Duncan is, in many ways, more her doing than his. What is most interesting about Macbeth, though, is not the clear connection between his 'character' and his actions, but the very lack of any such connection. There is in the play, no relation between emotion and action - Macbeth does not hate or despise those he kills. He has no grudge against Duncan or Banquo, least of all against Lady Macduff and her children. Macduff, indeed is the only person in the play who acts out of emotion - his hatred for Macbeth is real and fully motivated. Even the wronged Malcolm is cold and unemotional - everything we see or hear in the play emphasises his lack of deep inner feeling.

Indeed one of the most splendidly ironic scenes in the play (3, 1) plays on this whole concern for motives. Macbeth is hiring the murderers to kill Banquo. They are professional killers and we have no interest in them beyond the function they have to perform. They have nothing to say, no glorious lines of poetry, no subtle distinctions of character. We are about as interested in them as we are in the motives of a mafia hit-man: they do it for the money; that is all we know and all we need to know. And yet Macbeth insists on trying to supply them with a motive. Not content just to hire them to kill Banquo, he has to convince them - and in part himself - that they are repaying Banquo for past wrongs, that this is all part of a mediaeval revenge drama. He goes off on flights of rhetoric, more for their own sake, than for any real effect on the murderers: when they look like joining in the game with the beginnings of a rhetorical answer (127) he cuts them off. Their response, for the most part, is perfunctory, but they recognise this as a charade they must go through, as a part of pleasing the customer:

> *Macbeth: Both of you*
> *Know Banquo was your enemy.*
> *Murderers: True, my lord. (3, 1, 113 -)*

If they were really stirred up by hatred, really convinced of the motive that Macbeth invents for them, they would launch into some formal expression of their emotions. But there is no railing, no denunciation, merely a "True my lord." The scene shows us a world in which motives themselves have become inventions, a kind of formal fiction. It should be obvious that the play works from something else, from some other set of dramatic tensions than individual motivations.

6. If the play isn't about Macbeth's ambitions, does that mean he's just a psychopath?

What *Macbeth* gives us instead of a moral tale about ambition is a struggle between Macbeth's desire to make his own destiny - the desire of the new world - and the rule-bound social order in which he lives. What is so powerful about *Macbeth* is the extent to which that struggle, in the play, is dramatised in ritual terms, through images of magic, of occult ceremonies, of witches, of unborn children. If Macbeth is a man in transition, then the things that speed him to his doom are the transitional things of rituals.

The witches are half-human, half-otherworldly, their brew is full of those slippery, reptilian creatures that have altered significance because they are neither one thing nor the other, neither fish nor flesh, but slip between the categories: toads, snakes, newts, frogs, bats, adders, blindworms, lizards. And Macbeth, in his imagery, thinks of Banquo and Fleance the same way - he compares them to a snake and a worm (3, 2, 13 and 3, 4, 29) and connects them to the venom that the witches use in their brew (3, 4, 30). He also connects them in his mind to scorpions and bats (3, 2). The linking of these half-and-half creatures to the dangers that Macbeth sees around him - Banquo and Fleance - an imagery that becomes real with the final assault on the castle by the half-men/half-trees (Birnam Wood come to Dunsinane), is the dramatic medium by which the confusion of Shakespeare's own times is made concrete in the play.

7. Why does Macbeth get so obsessed with Fleance, and why is Macduff not of woman born?

The most powerful of these ritualistic images in the play is that of the unborn child. In most traditional societies the unborn child is dangerously ambiguous and therefore of great ritual significance. The anthropologist Mary Douglas writes about the unborn child as belonging to the group of "people who are somehow kept out of the patterning of society, who are placeless. They may be doing nothing wrong, but their status is indefinable...The unborn child's present position is ambiguous, its future equally so. For no one will say what sex it will have or whether it will survive the hazards of infancy. It is often treated as both unbearable and dangerous...Danger lies in transitional states, simply because transition is neither one state nor the next, it is indefinable."

This notion that the unborn child was both dangerous and powerful - and therefore in need of being dealt with ritually - was a very live issue in Shakespeare's time. The belief that the unborn child was an evil spirit possessed by the devil had been the standard one, leading to the ceremony of baptism being conducted in conjunction with an exorcism of the child. At the church door the priest blew three times into the face of the child and said "Go out of him unclean spirit, and give place to the Holy Ghost the comforter." This practice had been officially dropped by the Protestants only in 1552 but it was still being hotly debated in Shakespeare's day with assertions such as that of the Vicar of Ashford, Kent, that unbaptised infants were the firebrands of Hell. The important point is that, in Shakespeare's world, the unborn child is recognised as supremely ambiguous, a powerful image of transition from one world to another, both innocent and dangerous, both vulnerable and powerful.

This is why images of unborn children run through *Macbeth*. Macbeth himself, by killing Duncan and rebelling against feudal order, makes himself one of those people who are left out of the patterning of society, who are placeless. He puts himself into the territory of the unborn children and they literally haunt him. In Lady Macbeth's shocking image the tenderness of the infant child turns to horrible violence:

> *I would while it was smiling in my face,*
> *Have plucked my nipple from his boneless jaws*
> *And dashed the brains out...(1, 7, 54-)*

Thereafter, unborn children, both dreadful and innocent, surround Macbeth. There is the witches':

> *Finger of birth-strangled babe*
> *Ditch-delivered by a drab... (4, 1, 30-1)*

which echoes Lady Macbeth's image. There is, most importantly, the line of unborn kings of Scotland, Banquo's unborn heirs, who are as central to the play as any living character because they dominate Macbeth's thoughts for most of the action. The "bloody child" conjured onto the stage before us makes this danger to Macbeth physically present. And it links this line of unborn children to the other "unborn child" who haunts Macbeth, Macduff. It is the "bloody child" who tells Macbeth that "none of woman born" will harm him (4, 1, 80 -). Macduff is literally "unborn" in the sense that the play quibbles on the word "born" - he has not been born in the conventional manner. And in his confrontation with Macbeth it is his status as an infant that allows him to win out. Macbeth who has made himself like the unborn children - transitional, dangerous, yet curiously innocent, neither one thing nor the other - is eventually undone by them.

8. Why are there three witches and three murderers?

In this ritualised world, nothing will stay still. Good and bad, life and death, appearance and reality break out of their boundaries and turn into their opposites. Physically, the witches embody the spirit of Shakespeare's times: "What seemed corporal melted/ As breath into the wind." (1, 3, 81) and this description of them could be a motto for the whole play. Whereas in a fixed world, everything is divided into two - good and bad, life and death, male and female - and so on, in *Macbeth* there is always a third that is neither one thing nor the other. In some cases, twos literally keep turning into threes. In Act 1, scene 7, Macbeth is musing on his "double trust" towards Duncan, but this double becomes treble as he describes it: "I am his kinsman and his subject...(and) his host." Banquo's murderers whom we meet as a pair, suddenly become for no good reason, three (3, 3). The witches speak in three parts ("Show!/ Show!/ Show!") and make much of the number 3 ("Thrice the brinded cat hath mewed."), and show three apparitions - making Macbeth imagine he has three ears: "Had I three ears I'ld hear thee." (4, 1, 78).

Right from the start, in fact, not only is fair foul and foul fair, but it is difficult to keep our minds on who is good and who is bad. We will learn, crudely, that Macbeth is evil and Banquo good, but before we meet them we have had them confused in our minds. The Captain's speeches (1, 2) and Duncan's questions make "Macbeth" and "Macbeth and Banquo" virtually interchangeable terms. More than this, the loyal Macbeth is virtually indistinguishable from the traitor Macdonwald. The latter is called "merciless" but it is Macbeth whom we hear of as being merciless and the image is of them as "two spent swimmers that do cling together." Even in praising Macbeth and Banquo the Captain says it is as if "they meant to memorize another Golgotha", associating them with the crucifiers of Christ, hardly a comforting image of goodness. We also have opposites, comfort and discomfort, being confused: "whence comfort seems to come/ Discomfort swells." And then a traitor's name - Thane of Cawdor - being given to the greatest of the loyal soldiers, Macbeth. Hardly any wonder that the witches chant of "Double, double" is echoed here by the Captain -"As cannons overcharged with double cracks/So they doubly redoubled strokes upon the foe." (1, 2, 37-8). A basic description of the background to what will follow has become uncomfortably elusive, making what should be easy opposites, two sides in a battle, uneasy and shifty.

9.   What is a man?

Simple things that shouldn't need defining at all become the subject of endless quibbling, of ifs and buts. We know, broadly speaking, what a man is, but in the slippery world of *Macbeth* it becomes hard to tell what a man is or isn't. Macbeth, having decided not to kill Duncan, maintains that anyone who would do so would cease to be a man:

> *I dare do all that may become a man;*
> *Who dares do more is none. (1, 4, 47)*

And he is right, for once he has killed Duncan, even the simple word "man" starts to collapse and turn to nothing. At the beginning of the third act, one of the murderers, in conference with Macbeth about the plan to kill Banquo, utters the simple statement "We are men, my liege." (3, 1, 92) Macbeth refuses to accept the word "man" as meaning anything and immediately launches into a tirade in which the murderers are compared to dogs and dogs themselves are split into their kinds and shapes.

Shortly afterwards, faced with the ghost of Banquo, Macbeth is caught by his own prophecy and ceases to be a man in the eyes of his wife, and indeed, of himself. She describes him as "quite unmanned in folly". (3, 4, 73) She asks him "Are you a man?" (3, 4, 59) and he casts doubt on the answer with his "What man dare, I dare." (3, 4, 100) When the ghost disappears, he says of himself that "I am a man again", but the word has become so meaningless, so much a thing of nothing, that the statement, rather than restoring him to some fixed and well-defined state, serves only to mark the degree to which Macbeth himself has been cut adrift from recognisable limits.

And his disease is catching. In the next act, even his bitterest enemies start to sound like Macbeth on the subject of what a man is and does:

Malcolm: Dispute it like a man.
Macduff: But I must also feel it as a man. (4, 3, 219-)

As things fall apart, even the most basic of opposites, those of life and death, become fluid. As Macduff calls them to look at Duncan's murdered body, Malcolm and Banquo become ghosts rising from the dead, even though they are alive and well: "As from your graves rise up and walk like sprites." (2, 3, 81) Sleep becomes confused with death as "death's counterfeit" (2, 3, 78), as "the death of each day's life" (2, 2, 37). The dead Banquo takes his place at Macbeth's supper and Macbeth wonders how it is that the dead will not stay dead: "our graves must send/Those that we bury back...". (3, 4, 73-4) The sleepwalking Lady Macbeth (5, 1) is neither dead nor alive, but something in between. Malcolm and Macduff's cause, it is said, would "excite the mortified man", that is, stir up the dead. (5, 2, 4) Macduff fears that "my wife and children's ghosts will haunt me still." (5, 7, 16) And again, Macbeth himself senses this loss of a clear distinction between life and death early on, knowing that the dead Duncan will still be "alive" for himself, still shaping Macbeth's destiny and influencing everything that happens to him.

10.   Why do the witches foretell the future?

If the relationship between cause and effect, between something that has happened in the past and something that exists in the present is under stress in *Macbeth*, then so also is the relationship between the past and the future. This is the area of prophecy, and prophecy itself is a major concern of the play, as it was of Shakespeare's time.

Prophecies were taken seriously in Shakespeare's time, generally because they were a way of expressing the desire for political and social change, a desire that could not be expressed in any other language. The historian Keith Thomas makes this connection clear: "It was the existence of rebellious feeling which led to the circulation of prophecies...It was rebels who read into them an application to current events, and they did so because they wished to do so. At times of stress, men scrutinised these ancient myths with a view to extracting from them some sanction for the dangerous courses of action upon which they proposed to embark. Under the pressure of change they most felt the need for reassurance that what was happening had been foreseen by their ancestors and was in some sense part of a larger plan. It was no accident that the periods when prophecies were most prominent in English life were precisely those of rebellion, discontent and violent change...Prophecies disguised the break with the past." This could be an exact description of Macbeth, the violent rebel against the established order, and his relationship to the witches.

Not only prophecies, but prophecies that lead to civil disorder and that boomerang on those who believe in them were constantly in the air in Shakespeare's time. No rebellion by peasants and no treason trial was complete without reference to the traitors and rebels being spurred on by false prophets. And these prophecies were often bitterly ironic in exactly the way that the witches' prophecies in *Macbeth* are, seeming to offer victory, but in fact foretelling disaster. Rebellious peasants would go into battle at a certain place on foot of a prophecy that that place would be filled with dead bodies, not realising that the dead bodies would be their own. In the year before *Macbeth* was written, a gentleman could cite "26 ancient writers" in support of a prophecy that England would be torn apart by religious wars. Two years earlier, the same prophecies had been discussed by mourners at Queen Elizabeth's funeral. Far from being an exotic fantasy, the whole theme of prophecy in *Macbeth* is as topical to Shakespeare's audience as today's headlines are to us, and just as threatening and dangerous.

11. Does Macbeth believe them?

The important point about the prophecies in the play is not whether they are true or false, or whether Macbeth believes them or not, but that they are both true and false, that Macbeth both believes and does not believe them. Macbeth is a man in transition, the play is a play about a time of transition, and that is why it is a tragedy. And one of the things that is changing in that transition is the belief in ancient wisdom and prophecies. *Macbeth* is written in a century - the seventeenth - at the beginning of which it is taken for granted that everything was known in the past and that wisdom has only to be recovered, and at the end of which it is assumed that almost nothing was known in the past and everything has to be invented. Macbeth exists between one and the other, both believing in the kind of system in which everything is already known and can therefore be grasped by prophecy, and in the opposite of that, a world in which everything, including yourself, has to be made up as you go along, in which precedent and established order count for nothing.

Part of the "tragic flaw" idea of Macbeth is that he is unusually gullible, that he is too easily taken in by the witches, implying that prophecy itself must self-evidently be nonsense. But this is true neither to what we know of Macbeth himself nor to the dramatic force of the play. The very first time we hear of what Macbeth is like and what he does, it is the Captain telling us of Macbeth "Disdaining Fortune" (1, 2, 17), that is, mocking pre-ordained fate - the precise opposite of a man who is overly inclined to believe prophecies that tell him his fate has all been decided in advance. Even before Macbeth meets the witches at all, there are disturbing prophecies spoken unknowingly by others: Ross calls Macbeth "Bellona's bridegroom", (1, 2, 54) which is much truer than he thinks. Bellona is the goddess of war, and Macbeth, as we will see, is in fact married to a goddess of war, Lady Macbeth. Duncan gives Macbeth, the soon-to-be traitor, the title of the traitorous Thane of Cawdor. It is not in the first instance the devious witches who prophesy, but events and words spoken by others.

And this sense of unintentional prophecy continues throughout the play. Ross says that Macbeth being called Thane of Cawdor is "an earnest of a greater honour", (1, 3, 104) which it turns out to be, for it is the fact that he does become Thane of Cawdor that spurs Macbeth on to become king, which is indeed a greater honour, though not the one that Ross was thinking of. Macbeth's distracted conduct and rudeness towards Angus and Ross (1, 3) when they confirm a part of the witches' prophecy is itself a foreshadowing of the much more serious breach of civility and good manners in Act 3, scene 4 when Macbeth disrupts the supper on seeing the ghost of Banquo. Macduff's calling Banquo a ghost in Act 2, scene 3 is an unintentional prophecy of precisely what Banquo will be a few scenes later. In Act 4, scene 3, Macduff talks of "welcome and unwelcome things at once" (138) just before Ross comes in with the most unwelcome news imaginable - the slaughter of Macduff's wife and children. (Malcolm's tedious self-accusations in this scene coming as they do after we have seen so many things spoken in one sense turning out to be true in another, increases our sense of foreboding about how Malcolm will rule. Why will his heirs not succeed? Will something of what he says about his own depravity turn out to be true?)

What this means is that in the play things do happen as predicted, even when the predictions are unintentional and have nothing at all to do with the witches. Prophecy not only operates independently of the witches, it is also not identified exclusively with evil. For Edward the Confessor, an image of pure goodness in the play, is said to have " a heavenly gift of prophecy" (4, 3, 157). It is therefore quite reasonable for Macbeth to believe in prophecy and it is the events of the play and not his "character" which gives the prophecies their ironic weight.

It is important to remember that if Macbeth fully believed the witches' prophecies, there would be no tragedy. If he was a superstitious mediaeval man, he would take these supernatural portents at face value and assume, as he is tempted to do, that the prophecies will fulfil themselves without his having to take any action at all:

If chance will have me King, why, chance may crown me,
Without my stir. (1, 3, 143-)

It would be pointless to kill Duncan, and even more pointless to kill Banquo in an attempt to frustrate the second part of the prophecy. If, on the other hand, he were a modern rational man, he would discount the prophecies as gibberish or, as the Puritans in Shakespeare's time would have done, as the work of the devil. But he is neither one thing nor the other. Like a modern man he sees himself as the maker of his own fate. Like a mediaeval man, he is profoundly affected by the prophecies. He believes them when they tell him what he wants to hear, and disbelieves them when they do not. At the very moment when he is most in thrall to them - plotting the murder of Banquo because of them - he also announces his defiance of fate, of the notion of a pre-ordained future: "come, fate, into the list" (3, 1, 71). He is destroyed by being caught in the middle between two systems of belief.

It is significant that the individuals who haunt Macbeth by way of the witches' prophecies are themselves split and divided. He fears both Banquo and Fleance; he attacks both Macduff and Macduff's family. And the actions he takes on foot of the prophecies are themselves both double and doubly ironic. He gives the murderers a double task: to kill Banquo and to kill Fleance, and they carry out half of it. He sets out to kill Macduff and Macduff's family, and he achieves half of it. And in each case it is the wrong half. If he is to act on the prophecies, then he needs to kill Fleance and Macduff. What he manages to do is to kill Fleance's father, Banquo, and Macduff's son, the wrong father and the wrong son. The whole thing balances out neatly - he kills a father and a son - but the neatness is grotesquely wrong.

And this is one of the most remarkable things about *Macbeth*. We expect a tragedy - think, for instance, of *King Lear* or *Hamlet* - to end in chaos, with everything in a mess, having fallen apart more or less completely. If there is terror in these plays it is in the utter disorder of things. But *Macbeth* works differently. What is terrifying at the end of *Macbeth* is not how disorderly things are but how orderly. Everything, especially those things which seem impossible, fits together neatly. Birnam Wood does come to Dunsinane. Macduff is not of woman born.

In this, *Macbeth* is the closest of Shakespeare's plays to the old Greek tragedies with which his work is often, wrongly, compared. The sense of a prophecy being fulfilled in unexpected ways, of a coincidence that is disturbing because it is too neat is like that of the Greek tragedy *Oedipus Rex* by Sophocles, where the hero discovers that by a grotesque string of coincidences and in fulfilment of a prophecy, he has married his own mother. In *Macbeth*, Shakespeare, like Sophocles before him, plays on something that we know from our daily lives: that coincidences, things fitting together too neatly, far from being orderly and comforting, are deeply disturbing because they remind us of disorder. When things fit together purely by chance, as they do in *Macbeth* and in the coincidences of our daily lives, they remind us of how powerful chance is, of how even the most unlikely things are likely to happen. Far from convincing us that there is a pattern and an order to everything, coincidences make us feel that everything is random, that meaning and significance occur only through a meaningless accident.

This is the sense that we get at the end of the play. The neatness of everything arises out of the meaninglessness and disorder that are all around. We have just heard from Macbeth in the "Tomorrow, and tomorrow, and tomorrow" speech (5, 5, 17-) one of the most powerful evocations of meaninglessness in all of literature. The whole state of Scotland is in chaos. Foul whisperings, as the Doctor says, are abroad. The order of nature itself has been upset. And then here we have this neat, orderly ending. The neatness is deliberately perverse, for it serves really to underline the absurdity of everything else.

For instance, the meaninglessness of Macbeth's death, and that of Lady Macbeth, is stressed by the neatness with which the death of Young Siward (5, 8) is rounded-off by being discussed, commented on and polished with the regulation words of praise. But this piece of neatness, this conventional tidying up, is in fact disturbingly out of place. We don't actually give a damn for Young Siward. He has appeared for at most two minutes in the fifth act, where his sole function has been as an adjunct to Macbeth, a necessary piece of stage furniture so that we can see Macbeth being defiant, fierce, his old military self again for a few minutes before his death. By neatly tying up Young Siward's death, Shakespeare stresses how appallingly casual have been the deaths of the two most interesting characters, for the audience, in the play, Macbeth and Lady Macbeth. It is neatness and order used to make us aware of disorder and chaos, in the same way that the neat coincidence of the witches' prophecies being fulfilled at the end serves not to make us satisfied at the symmetry of the conclusion, but to leave us disturbed and disconcerted.

The significant thing about all of this is that it makes us feel uncomfortable about order, pattern, things being in their proper place. Macbeth needing to kill a father and a son but killing the wrong father and the wrong son, the proper forms of marking a death being gone through but for the wrong character, the prophecies working out but in bizarre and unpredictable ways, all serve to undermine the whole idea of order itself. So while the things that happen in the play - the traitor being punished and the rightful succession to the throne being re-established - serve to uphold the values of order, duty, the proper patterns of feudal society, the way they happen serves to subvert those very values. This is the dramatic tension which is at the heart of the play, and it is because Macbeth is the focus for that tension that he is so interesting and so exciting. He contains within himself not just a "character", but a whole set of conflicts that embody a society and a history.

12. Is Malcolm boring?

Another way to get at this tension is through looking at Malcolm. Malcolm is the embodiment of the order that is to be restored, the play's location of active goodness. But there is an enormous tension for anyone watching the play between what we know about Malcolm and what we feel about him, between what he says and the way he says it. We know that he is good, but we feel that he is boring. We agree with what he says but wish he would either get on with it or say it with even a little of the poetic force Macbeth can manage. Morally, we are on his side, dramatically we are against him. We want him to win, but we don't want to have to listen to him. His "Oh, by whom?" on hearing of the death of his royal and beloved father writes him off as a man of emotional depth.

In Act 4, scene 3 he bores us to tears with his long-winded game of self-accusation, and this irritation on our part is clearly what Shakespeare intends. The scene is placed in such a way, immediately after the murder of Macduff's family, as to heighten its dull coyness when compared to the heart-stopping and heart-rending action we have just witnessed. We know what Macduff does not yet know and to see Malcolm tease him and torture him with his verbal game can only make Malcolm not merely boring but somewhat despicable in our eyes. And the quality of Malcolm's response to Macduff's grief can only reinforce this negative impression of him. It is as bad as his "Oh, by whom?", with Malcolm stupidly urging a stiff upper lip on a man whose life has just collapsed, offering no real human sympathy and attempting repeatedly to turn Macduff's pain to his own military purposes. Macduff's line, "He has no children" (4, 3, 216) is often taken as referring to Macbeth (thus giving rise to pointless arguments about how many children Lady Macbeth has) but it is far more likely that it is directed at Malcolm, a bitter put-down of the latter's shallow and insensitive pretence at knowing how to "cure this deadly grief".

Macbeth moves quickly and feels deeply; Malcolm moves slowly and has no capacity for deep feeling whatsoever. Even in the numerical symbolism of the play, it is noticeable that Malcolm is a lesser figure than Macbeth. Macbeth's twos become threes (his "double trust", three murderers and three ears, mentioned earlier), but Malcolm's twos become one. At the start of the play, he is part of a duo, seen always in tandem with his brother Donalbain. At the end of the play, he is, inexplicably, one - Donalbain, for some unknown reason, has disappeared. In more senses than one, we get the disturbing feeling that Malcolm has something missing.

With all this in mind it is particularly eerie that Malcolm's final speech, the one in which order is restored and the action is tied up, is almost an exact echo of Duncan's speech near the beginning of the play when the earlier battle is concluded, the succession to the throne is settled, a traitor beheaded (Macdonwald), rewards are promised and titles are given out. Malcolm speaks his last speech with a battle won, the succession to the throne settled, a traitor beheaded (Macduff has just come in with Macbeth's head) and in it he promises rewards and distributes titles. And we know what happened after Duncan's speech - instead of being a prelude to peace, order and a smooth handing-on of the crown, it was a prelude to treason, disorder and the seizing of the crown by Macbeth. Two things combine to make this echo eerie. One is the fact that throughout the play, we have seen things being foreshadowed in all sorts of unintentional ways, and we are by now used to the idea of accidental prophecies. The other is that the idea of an ending itself is one of the things that has been consistently denied throughout the play.

13.   Does the play end?

Early in the play (1, 7, 1-) Macbeth devotes a whole speech ("If it were done when 'tis done, then 'twere well/It were done quickly") to the question of whether an action can ever be finished. The speech is interrupted by Lady Macbeth and is itself left unfinished. It is also the beginning of a set of actions - the murder of Duncan - whose consequences will never be done with for Macbeth. The murder itself refuses to be finished in one go - Lady Macbeth has to go back with the knives. Duncan's blood will not wash off. The days will not end in sleep. Banquo refuses to die in two ways - he comes back as a ghost and he lives on, in a sense, in his children who will be kings hereafter. Macbeth cannot say "Amen", the word which finishes a prayer. (2, 2, 31) Macduff fears that his wife and children, though dead, will come back to haunt him if he does not revenge himself on Macbeth. Far from being given reason to believe that the end of the play is the end of the story, our experience in watching the play is that things refuse to end at all.

The point in all of this is that *Macbeth* is not a play which merely shows that order is good and disorder is bad. The order that is restored at the end of the play and the formal orderliness of the prophecies turning out to be true, are, respectively weak and disturbing. Vicious, destructive and obsessive as he may be, Macbeth exists within an order that offers little in the way of a convincing alternative to him. Shakespeare shows us the cost of the disorder which Macbeth unleashes - the murders of innocent people, the ruin of Scotland - but also, in a sense, its necessity. It is not for nothing that Macbeth, through his use of the witches' prophecies, is identified with the social rebels of Shakespeare's time, with their inevitable but inevitably doomed rebellions. Like them, he is caught in a time of disturbing change in which he can do little except rebel. Like them, too, he cannot win. He is forced into an act which is out of its place in history, into a desire for which there is no possible fulfillment.

14.   How does Macbeth, who is in many ways so appalling a figure, come to be someone who can seem to represent, not just himself, but a whole human dilemma and a whole sense of history?

Surely we would prefer to see him as an isolated madman, which is what he has become by the end of the play, than to take him as representing us and, in certain moments, speaking for us. The answer is that we would prefer to do just this, but the play does not let us do so. It is partly that, as we have mentioned, the alternatives to Macbeth in the play - Duncan, Banquo, Malcolm - are so bland and so boring that they make his passion, speed and awareness of himself all the more attractive.

The one passionate and strong alternative to Macbeth, Macduff, is temperamentally inclined to keep out of nasty situations - he absents himself from Macbeth's coronation and isn't around when the murderers come for his family - and is stirred to vigorous action only by hatred and the desire for revenge. He acts out of an immediate and personal cause, whereas Macbeth is impelled to go against his personal instincts and engage himself with things that are so big and general that they are impossible for him to pin down: the future, the supernatural, the forces that control human destiny. Macduff operates in a small world, Macbeth, for all his obsessive violence, operates in a very big one.

For what Macbeth is concerned about more than anything else is the future, and this is what is really remarkable about him. Most of us live day by day and think of the future, if at all, only occasionally and in the abstract. It is not, to us, real. Macbeth's curse is that it is real for him, often more real than the present. The witches give him a little taste of the future and it becomes addictive. As the play goes on, it becomes more and more important to him, blotting out the present almost completely. His present life, his achievement of the position of King of Scotland, is of no consequence to him. What he craves is to control the future, to be the father of kings who will rule long after he is dead. The obsession reaches such a point that when something immediate and dramatic happens to him in the present - the death of Lady Macbeth - he immediately wishes it were part of the future: "She should have died hereafter". (5, 5, 17) Lady Macbeth set out to feel the future in the present ("I feel now/The future in the instant." (1, 5, 56), but in the end Macbeth's feelings for her are obliterated by the future and his obsession with it.

15. Why does this sense of the future take such a hold over Macbeth?

The reasons have to do with his sense of his own time in history. He kicks against his own time and its values of order and hierarchy and duty. He wants to be free to act on his desires, though he has no concrete sense of what those desires really are. But he knows, too, that he cannot do this in the present, that the time and the place in which he lives simply don't work like that. So what he wants is to live in a future time. He wants to control the future by being the father of its rulers. He wants, in a sense, to be his own descendants. This is why it is much more important to him that he succeed in killing Fleance than it was to kill Duncan. The present - being king

- matters only as a stepping-stone to the future. It is important to be king not in itself but because only a king can found a dynasty which will control the future.

This, too, is the reason why time haunts him so much. Time runs through the play like a seam of ore. The second act begins with Banquo asking Fleance what time it is, and is punctuated by a kind of ticking clock - the bell rings to signal that it is time for the killing of Duncan and rings again when the act is discovered. Then time starts to go wrong. It is day by the clock, says Ross, (2, 4, 6-7) and yet "dark night strangles the travelling lamp". From now on time gets in everywhere and is spoken of as an actor in the drama itself, a force that has been let loose: "fill up the time", "let every man be the master of his time", "the perfect spy o' th' time", "the pleasure of the time", the "last syllable of recorded time". The last speech of the play uses the word "time" three times, and, remarkably, when Macduff holds up the head of Macbeth, he doesn't say "Scotland is free" or "we are free", but "The time is free." (5, 8, 55)

And the line makes sense. For Macbeth's obsession with the future, his desire to make himself part of some other time than his own, has been an attempt to capture time and bring it under his command. When he can't do this, he tries to destroy time altogether. Like all tyrants, he wants to destroy what he cannot control. His own reaction to Lady Macbeth's death brings home to him his failure to control the future, for in spite of his desire that she should have died in the future, she hasn't done so. So he conjures up a vision in which time is obliterated, in which one day becomes the same as the next, and therefore there is no such thing as past, present and future. All three are meshed together in one meaningless whole:

To-morrow, and to-morrow, and to-morrow
Creeps in this petty pace from day to day
To the last syllable of recorded time... (5, 5, 19-)

But, and this is the other main reason why the play does not permit us to distance ourselves from Macbeth, his vain and hopeless desire to live in the future, to be alive in a time where he would not be trapped by the rules of history and the confines of his own time's values, is something that we all, in some sense, share. Because there has never been a perfect world, a world that would match our desires, and because we all dream sometime that such a world might exist in the future, we share his attraction to that future. Like the

peasants of Shakespeare's time who revolted against the order of
the day and cited prophecies as their excuse, Macbeth is a rebel
whose cause can only make sense long after he is dead. That is his
tragedy and also, to a degree, ours.

16.   What about the soliloquies?

It is Macbeth's great speeches that make this connection between
us and him, for, in spite of surface appearances, they are not the
purely private, inner thoughts of an isolated man. Indeed, one of the
most extraordinary things that Shakespeare does in the play is to
break down the whole notion of what is internal and what is external.
In the early part of the play, the difference between our inner selves
(our hearts) and our outer, public selves (our faces) is a major
concern of the imagery: "There's no art/To find the mind's
construction in the face."; "look like th' innocent flower,/But be the
serpent under't."; "False face must hide what the false heart doth
know." When so many other differences - between fair and foul,
truth and lies, men and women - are breaking down, this is the
difference that is insisted on - between what we are inside and what
we look like to other people.

But it is a distinction that is set up so clearly only to be knocked
down all the more forcefully. *Macbeth* is indeed full of soliloquies
- 15 per cent of it is monologue, as compared with just 5 per cent
of *Hamlet* - and Macbeth does become very obviously isolated, as
he tells us himself in "My way of life/ Is fall'n into the sear, the
yellow leaf..." But there is nothing private or internal about these
soliloquies. Instead, Shakespeare develops a way of speaking in
which there is no distinction between the internal thoughts and
feelings of a character and the outward expression of these feelings,
or where at the very least that distinction is made unclear. We are
made used to this kind of speech in two scenes: that of Banquo's
ghost and the sleepwalking scene.

The words that Macbeth speaks to Banquo's Ghost in Act 3, scene
4 are both internal speech and external speech. From the point of
view of everyone but Macbeth, they are a soliloquy - a man talking
to himself, expressing his inner thoughts. Because they cannot see
the Ghost, they cannot see that he is addressing those words to

someone in particular. But from the point of view of Macbeth, these words are not soliloquy but dialogue: they are addressed directly to the ghost and expect an answer. Thus they are at one and the same time inner and outer, demolishing the distinction between these two which has been so carefully established earlier.

This is taken, if anything, further in the sleepwalking scene, where Lady Macbeth's private, internal thoughts, so private that she is not herself even conscious of saying them out, are overheard and discussed by the Doctor and the Waiting Woman. They are even written down and recorded by the Doctor.

And almost immediately after this scene we have Macbeth speaking out his most private thoughts, again overheard by the Doctor. The soliloquy at Act 5, scene 3, line 22 - ("My way of life etc") which is more nakedly self-revealing and self-critical than any in the play is not properly speaking a soliloquy at all, for it is spoken before an on-stage audience. We could call it public speech, except that by now the distinction between what is public and what is private has completely disappeared. And this is followed by the "To-morrow, and to-morrow, and to-morrow" speech, which takes the process to its final point.

Surrounded by his soldiers and his battle flags, Macbeth gives expression to his deepest internal feelings, his most profoundly personal sentiments. But he does not use the word "I" or talk about himself. He uses the word "our" and talks about humanity. His vision of humanity may come out of his personal situation, it may be bleak, but the humanity which he speaks of is still a common humanity. And there is no longer the possibility of deceit. The heart can now be read in the face, the mind's construction emerges directly in the spoken word. What was not possible at the beginning of the play - to know what someone thinks and feels from what they say and do - has become not only possible, but unavoidable. For at least one moment in time, a man's inner self is not denied and refuted by the external world of history and power and violence. It is a moment that cannot last and that is quickly swallowed up by the forces of power and order and the values of Macbeth's own time, represented by Macduff and Malcolm and their troops. If we are glad to see Macbeth go, we are also glad to have had that moment.

3

Hamlet: Dying as an Art

1.   Hamlet is a slob, right?

Hamlet is a slob, a shirker. He has a job to do and won't do it, keeps persuading himself that there is some good reason for not getting on with it. He is certainly unwell and possibly evil. The problem of *Hamlet* is Hamlet. Hamlet is there to teach us a lesson: when faced with a difficult and unpalatable task we must stiffen our upper lips, put our consciences in the deep freeze and get on with it. Otherwise we shall surely come to a bad end.

Alternatively: yes, Hamlet is guilty of delay and indecision, but this is a flaw in an essentially noble nature. He is a melancholy intellectual in black tights, leaning up against a headstone with a skull in his hand. The play happens not in the castle at Elsinore but in the soul of Hamlet. It is a beautiful soul, far too beautiful to be fouled with something as vulgar as action. "A beautiful, pure, noble and most moral nature, without the strength of nerve which makes the hero, sinks beneath a burden which it can neither bear nor throw off", writes the German poet Goethe. Hamlet is a "pale cavalier" writes the French poet Arthur Rimbaud. Hamlet becomes gorgeous, dressed in feathered hat and velvet clothes. He wraps his hand in a silk handkerchief before he picks up the skull in the graveyard. His fashion accessories, like his soul, are the height of melancholy chic. The nineteenth century French painter Eugene Delacroix publishes a series of illustrations of Hamlet - young, delicate, beautifully pensive, his face devoid of passion, sarcasm, vulgarity. Critics start to write of performances of actors playing the part of Hamlet, not in relation to how well they match Shakespeare's play, but how well they match Delacroix's illustrations.

These two versions of *Hamlet* are two sides of the one coin, and in both Hamlet becomes uninteresting, either a slob or a poseur. Neither, as it happens, has very much to do with Shakespeare's play. Both have a lot to do with the need to prove that *Hamlet* is a tragedy of the Aristotelian sort, that it is about Tragic Heroes and Tragic Flaws and Inevitability. Hamlet posed great problems for the Tragic Hero men, for he is patently not a hero. He doesn't do what the Tragic Hero is supposed to do - fall from the top of Fortune's wheel to the bottom. Instead, he is at a low ebb when we first see him and continues on the same plane throughout the play. Far from being a play with the logic of inevitability running through it, *Hamlet* is extraordinarily illogical, full of plays-within-plays, sea journeys, graveyards, pirates, drownings, madnesses. Far from the ending having the neat feeling of fated retribution, it is a wild and messy heap of bodies, sordid and nasty, the result of "purposes mistook". If *Hamlet* was to be rescued for the irrelevant Aristotelian definition of tragedy, only one thing remained - the Tragic Flaw. More than any of the other tragedies, *Hamlet* has been explained in terms of the Tragic Flaw and more than any of the others it has been obscured.

2. Did this idea of Hamlet die out in the nineteenth century?

The idea that the character of Hamlet is the only thing really worth looking at in the play and that his character, whether noble or evil is essentially flawed, is one which has been extraordinarily persistent in the way that *Hamlet* has been written about, directed and taught. It is the main line of *Hamlet* criticism, running from Richardson, Goethe, Coleridge, Schlegel and Hazlitt, through the psychoanalytic movement to the present day. The question is Hamlet's delay in doing what he ought to do and the answer must lie in Hamlet's psychology. The last thing that needs to be done is look at *Hamlet* as a play and as Shakespeare's play.

What all of these views share is the idea that Hamlet is the problem, that he may indeed be evil. G. Wilson Knight, for instance, tells us that "To Hamlet comes the command of a great act - revenge... a sick soul is commanded to heal, to cleanse, to create harmony. But good cannot come of evil: it is seen that the sickness of his soul only further infects the state - his disintegration spreads out, disintegrating." Derek Traversi talks about "the disease, which emanating from Hamlet himself, expands from his wounded nature to cover the entire action." The doctrine of Original Sin which the notion of Tragic Flaw mirrors is given new life in Freudian psychoanalysis and Ernest Jones in his very influential study of Hamlet from a psychoanalytic point of view sees him as a sick patient on a consulting couch: "Throughout the play we have the clearest picture of man who sees his duty plain before him but who shirks it at every opportunity and suffers in consequence the most intense remorse."

What we end up with in this view is a clinical report on Hamlet which has almost nothing to do with the play: "Hamlet had, in years gone by, as a child, bitterly resented having to share his mother's affection even with his own father, had regarded him as a rival and had secretly wished him out of the way so that he might enjoy undisputed and undisturbed the monopoly of that affection... Without his being in the least aware of it, these ancient desires are ringing in his mind, are once more struggling to find conscious expression and need such an expenditure of energy again to repress them that he is reduced to the deplorable mental state he himself so vividly depicts." In this version of the play there are no soldiers, no political power struggles, no invading armies, no competing ideas about life and death and eventually not even a king who has killed Hamlet's father and usurped his throne. Claudius is nothing other than Hamlet himself: "He of course detests (Claudius) but it is the jealous detestation of one evil-doer towards his successful fellow...In reality his uncle incorporates the deepest and most buried part of his own personality, so that he cannot kill him without also killing himself. This solution is actually the one that Hamlet finally adopts."

3.   Sounds exciting. What's the problem?

All of this is absurd, because it involves ignoring the whole context and action of the play, but it only takes to a logical conclusion a long history of the interpretation of *Hamlet* in which the real play takes place in Hamlet's mind and everything else is irrelevant. But the view of Hamlet as at worst evil and at best mentally ill and defective in nerve and guts is still a very powerful one, even in the modern theatre. The American director Charles Marowitz writes that "I despise Hamlet. He is a slob, a talker, an analyser, a rationaliser. Like the parlour liberal or the paralysed intellectual, he can describe every facet of a problem, yet never pull his finger out. Is Hamlet a coward, as he himself suggests, or simply a poseur, a frustrated actor who plays the scholar, the courtier and the soldier as an actor (a very bad actor) assumes a variety of different roles? And why does he keep saying everything twice? And how can someone talk so pretty in such a rotten country with the sort of work he's got cut out for him? You may think he's a sensitive well-spoken fellow, but, frankly, he gives me a pain in the ass."

Or, less bluntly, the British director Jonathan Miller puts it like this: "I have always been interested in the idea of Hamlet as a rather unattractive character, a tiresome, clever, destructive boy who is very intelligent but volatile, dirty-minded and immature. This interpretation does not subvert the intelligence of the speeches even though we are usually given the noble Dane as a philosophical and restrained character whose reluctance to revenge is prompted by a fastidious refusal to indulge in bloody and inelegant actions. It may well be that he is also a childish creature full of tantrums and resentments who, in a purely Freudian way, is reluctant to kill the object that he seems to hate because by keeping Claudius, the object of his hatred, alive he can ignore the person he might have loathed even more - his father...Hamlet can then indulge in self-deluding fantasies of affection for the dead father."

Both Marowitz and Miller are right. Seen in the way they want to see him, Hamlet is a pain in the ass and a tiresome boy. Luckily for us, Shakespeare wrote a rather different play. In particular he wrote a play in which Hamlet's delay is not the issue. Apart from the soliloquies, in which Hamlet sometimes struggles with himself about the duties he has and the options open to him, there are only two occasions in the play where Hamlet's failure or refusal to act is the issue. The first is the single occasion when he actually rejects an opportunity to kill Claudius. And the second is when the ghost endorses his suggestion that he is "tardy". But in both cases, it is Hamlet's conception of his role, of what he must do and how he must do it, that is in question, not the mere idea of delay.

And Shakespeare deliberately gives us two alternative role models for Hamlet, both of which are weak and ineffectual. He has Hamlet contemplate Young Fortinbras and his headlong rush to war and possible death. Fortinbras is a man of action who does not scruple about moral consequences. But we have also just heard that Fortinbras' quest is abject folly - "a little patch of ground", a "straw" (4, 4). Hamlet, in seeming to admire Fortinbras takes up this word "straw", this image of futility - "to find quarrel in a straw when honour's at stake". How could such a straw man as Fortinbras offer an acceptable model of action for Hamlet, who is so sceptical about the worth of all this blind courage and inflated ambition? And the other possible model, Laertes, who does what Hamlet will not do - drop all hesitancy and all scruple about the afterlife - is, at the time he does so, a fool, a tool of Claudius who, while he thinks he is exercising his free will is in fact being manipulated by a consummate politician. There is no model of action for Hamlet, no easy way for him to do what he is told to do by the ghost. What Shakespeare gives us is not a slob or a shirker, but a man of action (the man whom everyone turns to at the start of the play when there is a crisis, the man who can board a pirate ship, the man who has few scruples about killing those he sees as threatening him) who is concerned with how, not whether, to perform his task. He is concerned with perfecting his role on a very tricky and untrustworthy stage.

4. So what's rotten in the state of Denmark?

There is not a single character in *Hamlet*, with the possible exception of Young Fortinbras, who sees the political and social world in which he lives as being anything other than corrupt, rotten, sordid, nasty. And Young Fortinbras is both a fool and a liar, a man who is willing to sacrifice his own and other people's lives for the sake of a worthless piece of ground, who is willing to break a solemn political undertaking if he sees the opportunity of power and advantage in doing so. *Hamlet* is unusual among Shakespeare's plays in that it has no stated ideal of good government, no great vision of the social order which has been disrupted. Things have gone too far for people to fool themselves. The king Claudius knows all about backhanders and bending the rules:

In the corrupted currents of this world
Offense's gilded hand may shove by justice,
And oft 'tis seen the wicked prize itself
Buys out the law.   (3, 3, 57-)

The Prince, Hamlet, looks around him and sees little except injustice and tyranny:

Th' oppressor's wrong, the proud man's contumely
The pangs of despised love, the law's delay,
The insolence of office, and the spurns
That patient merit of th' unworthy takes...
(3, 1, 71-)

The Lord Chamberlain, Polonius, when he wants to advise his son how to protect himself in the world, takes it for granted that the world is a dangerous and untrustworthy place: be slow to make friends, don't let yourself be in anybody's debt, keep your ears open but, whatever you say, say nothing. (1, 3, 59-). The Lord Chamberlain's son, when he wants to advise his sister, takes it for granted that men are dangerous and untrustworthy: don't listen to fine words, don't be taken in, don't even show yourself to the moon or you'll be ruined, live in constant fear - "Fear it, Ophelia, fear it, my dear sister...". (1, 3, 30-)

The first thing we see in *Hamlet* is the jumpiness of the soldiers on the battlements. These are the king's guards, in the royal castle, the centre of power and administration in Denmark. And yet they are jittery, cautious, watchful. The first words we hear are the fretful "Who's there?" This is a place in which anyone might sneak up behind you, a play in which you have to be on your guard. Lovers in their intimate moments are watched from behind walls, a man saying his prayers is spied on. Everything may be overheard. People hide behind curtains and pillars. Bedrooms and the palace itself can be invaded at any moment by an angry son, an angry mob, a conquering army. "The architecture of Elsinore" as Grigori Kozintsev has put it "does not consist of walls but of the ears which the walls have. There are doors, the better to eavesdrop behind, windows the better to spy from. The walls are made up of guards. Every sound gives birth to echoes, repercussions, whispers, rustling." In *Macbeth*, when a ghost comes to visit Macbeth, no one else can see him. It is a private moment in a public situation. In

Hamlet, when a ghost comes to see the Prince, everyone else sees it, indeed everyone else knows about it before Hamlet does. In *Hamlet* no one is every really surprised by anything that happens. It merely confirms what they already suspect. In *Hamlet*, even when a dead man's bones are found in a grave, everything is already known about who he is he, what he was like, what he did for a living. In *Hamlet* even when a ghost reveals his terrible secret which he has come all the way from the other side of death to reveal, it turns out to be no more than a confirmation ("O," says Hamlet when he hears that Claudius killed his father, "my prophetic soul.") In the world of *Hamlet*, when the King of Denmark sends a secret letter to the King of England, it is opened, tampered with, its contents altered. Nothing is secret, nothing private. *Hamlet* is about the most public play it is possible to imagine. The fact that it has become the very type of the private play, a play that takes place within a man's private thoughts, is a mark of the distortions that have befallen it over time.

Hamlet has come to be thought of as a play of soliloquies, a play dominated by a man talking to himself. In fact, *Hamlet* is in no way exceptional for the amount of monologue it has. Eight per cent of it is monologue - there is almost twice as much monologue in *Macbeth* which is generally thought of as a play full of incident and action. Hamlet's own soliloquies are six per cent of the play, and only half of these involve him using the word "I". Many of the soliloquies, including those like the "To be or not to be" speech which are thought of as being the most isolated and internal, use the word "we", and are opened out onto a vision of the society in which Hamlet lives, placing Hamlet among, not apart from, his fellow men.

Hamlet is a play in which there is neither privacy nor trust. What is more, in *Hamlet*, it is not just in court that the idea of trust, of proper order, has broken down. Claudius calls the ordinary people "the distracted multitude" and he tells Laertes that he has reason to fear them, that he can't just get rid of Hamlet because the people love him. Claudius talks of "the people muddied,/Thick and unwholesome in their thoughts and whispers". (4, 5, 81) The ordinary people, too, are thinking dark thoughts, whispering on the streets. Hamlet remarks to Horatio that social distinctions are breaking down, that it is getting hard to tell the difference between a peasant and a lord: "By the lord, Horatio, this three years I have taken note of it, the age is grown so picked that the toe of the peasant comes so near the heel of the courtier he galls his kibe." (5, 1, 130) And as the play goes on, the ordinary people become more and more threatening, more and more of a player in the drama. They want a new world, a world in which accepted hierarchy will be forgotten, and they follow Laertes to the very doors of Claudius' office with their clamouring:

> *The rabble call him lord;*
> *And as the world were but now to begin,*
> *Antiquity forgot, custom unknown,*
> *The ratifiers and props of every word,*
> *They cry 'Choose we; Laertes shall be king.'*
> *(4, 5, 98-)*

The old order has sunk into corruption, tyranny and decay, has become a world in which the individual is crowded out by the overweening demands of a dying state. The new order is frightening - the mob howling at the door, all customs thrown out, all promises broken. The Gentleman who reports on the rabble imagines it to be like a terrifying sea sweeping over the land, a fierce and elemental force blotting out all features, all individuality. And, most significantly he describes it as a breaking of boundaries: "overpeering of his list". The breaking of boundaries is dangerous, it is what threatens identity, individuality. Hamlet's tragedy is that he is caught between this old order and this new one, sharing some of the values of both, desperately trying to keep some individuality alive.

5.   But you can't deny that *Hamlet* is pretty morose?

Hamlet indeed is a play about death. Or rather, it is a play about the survival of the individual in the face of death. But this is not a metaphysical or mystical problem, and it's not just about Hamlet's psychology. It is not about a man in black tights looking into the empty eye sockets of a skull. It is a real question, rooted in the life of Shakespeare's time. Shakespeare and his contemporaries would have lived with death that was everyday and everywhere. There had always been death, of course, death in great numbers and death at an early age, but what is different in Shakespeare's time is the sense that this might not be the normal and natural state of affairs, that death was a real loss. What you have in Shakespeare's time, is on the one hand an educated elite and on the other hand a condition of life for the overwhelming majority of people which is characterised by pain, sickness and premature death. Even among the nobility, whose chances of living a long life were better than those of the poor, the life expectation at birth of boys was less than 30. Today it would be 70. "We shall find more who have died within thirty or thirty-five years of age than passed it" wrote a contemporary of Shakespeare's. Even those who survived could expect a great deal of physical pain, since very many people suffered from some chronic illness or other, at least in part because of poor diet. Epidemics were common and disastrous - when Shakespeare was in London in 1593, 15,000 people died of the plague; in 1603, 30,000, or over a sixth of the city's population, died. Poverty, sickness and sudden disaster were the most familiar features of the social environment. The difference now was that you had, for the first time, a reasonably large educated elite which was beginning to think that these things might not have to be the norm of life. In this fact lies the seed of a tragic vision, the vision that is at the heart of *Hamlet*.

Hamlet himself, we know, is a humanist. He is a member of the new educated elite, has been to Wittenberg University, is full of the new philosophy of his time. He sees every man as a potential god, is almost convinced of the Renaissance glorification of his species. But he is also inescapably aware of death, of its power to reduce all of this to nothing. "What a piece of work is man", he says, "how noble in reason, how infinite in faculties; in form and moving, how express and admirable, in action how like an angel,in apprehension how like a god: the beauty of the world, the paragon of animals!" But then, remembering death, he immediately adds "And yet to me what is this quintessence of dust?" (2, 2, 300-) Hamlet cannot think of life without thinking of death, of death without thinking of life. (It is a mark of the distortion of Shakespeare's play, the obsession with Hamlet's psychology as opposed to what he actually thinks, that in the most widely seen version of the play this century, Laurence Olivier's film of it, this whole speech about man is simply cut out.) What is dangerous and powerful about *Hamlet* is that it blurs the boundaries of two of our most basic categories - life and death. By the time the play is over, it is hard for us to tell one from the other.

Every Shakespearian tragedy involves death almost as a matter of course, as a part of the form. The tragic protagonist dies, and so do many others who get caught up, sometimes in the most peripheral way, in the action. But *Hamlet* is different. At the very outset of Macbeth's tragic course, he dismisses all thought of the life to come. For Othello, suicide in the grand tragic manner, is a natural escape, a logical and relatively easy act. For Lear, death is a deliverance, a kindness. Death is what frames the action of these plays. But for Hamlet, death is the central fact of life. He doesn't just think about death, he thinks about what it would be like to be dead. The play keeps us thinking about death all the time, about what death does to the soul and to the body. Much of the action is about the moment of death, the proper circumstances of death, the rites that should attend it, the refusal of death and life to keep their places as opposites in our categorisation of experience.

Shakespeare's time is a time of random deaths, of young deaths, of mass deaths, of meaningless deaths. What Hamlet is looking for throughout the play, in a sense, is a meaningful death, death that is properly done, at the right time and place, death that has significance in the order of things, death that is remembered and spoken about and felt for. He is trying, in a sense, to marry his humanist understanding about the importance of every human life, the significance of humanity itself, with the obvious and inescapable fact of his world - that people die improperly, for no reason, without the true cause being known, without the proper rites being observed, without significance. If he cannot change the world he lives in, make it into one that is not so dominated by death, he can at least, he believes, order the deaths that happen, make them rational. He wants to shape the old chaotic and corrupt world according to the principles of the new rationality which he has learned at Wittenberg. And of course you cannot do this; you cannot live in one world according to the principles of another world. This is what we call tragedy.

6. Is Hamlet a New Man?

Hamlet is a man in transition from one world view to another. It is a mistake to see him entirely as an example of the New Man, as a full-blooded Renaissance intellectual. If he were, there would be no tragedy. He would not believe in the ghost, or he would use his rational faculties to tell himself that its demands are unreasonable, that they don't make sense. He would get out, go back to Wittenberg and wait for the already decaying state to fall asunder. But there is too much of the old order within himself, too much concern for its demands. On the one hand, we have in Hamlet a man who believes that everything is relative, that there are no absolute standards of value or morality: "there is nothing either good or bad but thinking makes it so" (2, 2, 246). The first words of his first soliloquy have a decidedly scientific ring about them; "melt, thaw and resolve itself into a dew". A man who believes that there is nothing good or bad except in the way that we see it, a man who can use scientific language, is not a man who should believe in fate, who should deny free will. And yet this is what Hamlet, even the relatively cool Hamlet of the first act, does. Shakespeare gives us a Hamlet who in the course of a few lines can say on the one hand that customs should be broken ("it is a custom/More honoured in the breach than the observance"), that men should think for themselves and not be bound by what is traditional - the words of a Renaissance humanist - and then say that men are born with certain defects, that Nature or Fortune determines their characters and that there is nothing that they can do about it:

> So oft it chances in particular men
> That (for some vicious mole of nature in them,
> As in their birth, wherein they are not guilty,
> Since nature cannot choose his origin)
> By the o'ergrowth of some complexion,
> Oft breaking down the pales and forts of reason,
> Or by some habit that too much o'erleavens
> The form of plausive manners - that (these men
> Carrying, I say, the stamp of one defect,
> Being nature's livery, or fortune's star)
> Their virtues else, be they as pure as grace,
> As infinite as man may undergo,
> Shall in general censure take corruption
> From that particular fault. (1, 4, 23-)

In Shakespeare's tragedies, the real New Men, the real believers in the new philosophy, like Edmund in *King Lear*, laugh at the idea of astrology and at those who believe in it. To them, the idea of your fate and your character being determined at your birth is a foolish superstition. But Hamlet both believes it and doesn't believe it. This is the contradictory Hamlet who takes his father's ghost's orders seriously enough to say that he doesn't care if he dies in carrying them out, and who then does not execute them.

This is the Hamlet who says that theatre is a lie and then says that it can reveal the truth, the Hamlet who laughs at the idiocy of Young Fortinbras and then says that he should try to be more like him. This is the Hamlet who believes that he can deal in a world of death and yet bring order to it, the man who would try to make the irrational reasonable. It is the contradictions of his time, embodied in his own thinking, which makes for Hamlet's delay, not his desire to sleep with his mother or his tragic flaw as a shirker. By accepting his duty to kill and then trying to make that killing significant in all the proper details, Hamlet is trying to keep a foot in each of two contradictory worlds, to use the ideas of one for the sordid tasks of the other. It is hardly surprising that he fails for so long.

7. How does he keep a foot in each of two worlds?

The main way in which Hamlet tries to keep a foot in both worlds is through the idea of death itself. It is important to realise that one of the things that has become slippery and shifting in Shakespeare's time as one world view gives way to another is the very idea of the significance of death. One way of looking at death is giving way to another and Hamlet, tragically, looks at it both ways. Before the sixteenth century, the prevailing mediaeval notion of death is that it is familiar, inevitable and ordained by God. Death was to be accepted so long as it was not sudden, so long as it had some predictability about it. Sudden death, as Philippe Aries put it "destroyed the order of the world in which everyone believed; it became the absurd instrument of chance, which was sometimes disguised as the wrath of God." Thus, sudden, unexpected deaths were regarded as ignominious and shameful. "In this world that was so familiar with death, a sudden death was a vile and ugly death; it was frightening; it seemed a strange and monstrous thing that nobody dared talk about." Hamlet, with his obsession with the manner of his father's death, its furtive, secret, sudden and unprepared nature, seems to follow this mediaeval notion of death. He seems to be a part of the old world.

But this notion was changing precisely at the time that Shakespeare was writing. For the new men and the new religion, the moment of death itself was not important and should not be dwelt upon. In 1561, the English Puritan Thomas Becon writes that the pangs of death have been lingered over too lovingly by mediaeval rhetoric. Dying is a natural phenomenon that should not be dramatised. "It is not therefore at the moment of one's death or in the presence of death that one should think about death; it is throughout one's life... The art of dying was replaced by the art of living... a life dominated by the thought of death."

And this, too, is Hamlet. He, too, lives a life dominated by the thought of death. He is part of this new world and its ideas about death. He is mediaeval and modern, old and new. He is obsessed in a mediaeval way with the moment of death, in a modern way with the idea that death is something that should be present in our minds throughout our lives, making us contemptuous of life's achievements, as Hamlet himself is. Instead of being one thing or the other, he is both. On the issue which dominates the play he is fatally ambivalent. How, then, could he act in a simple, straightforward manner?

The first argument in *Hamlet*, the first clash between Hamlet and his enemies, is an argument about death. Hamlet is grieving over his father. Claudius and Gertrude believe that he is grieving too long. "How is it" asks Claudius "that the clouds still hang on you?" Gertrude confronts Hamlet with a mediaeval notion of human death- that it is common, ordinary, natural, only to be expected, not something to make too much fuss over:

Thou know'st 'tis common. All that lives must die,
Passing through nature to eternity. (1, 2, 72-)

What Gertrude and Claudius are saying is something that reflects reality in Elizabethan England - that people die all the time, that it is no big deal. Implicit in what Gertrude says is that there is no great difference between the death of a man and the death of an animal. Her attitude is like that of the Gravedigger which will so unsettle Hamlet much later in the play: "Custom hath made it in him a property of easiness", so that he sings while he is digging a grave."(5, 1, 64) Both in the first and the last acts of the play, there are those to whom death is something that you just get used to.

Claudius here, though, goes further than Gertrude and stresses that death is a matter of nature taking its course and that in grieving too long Hamlet is challenging the whole feudal order, the whole sense that certain things are right and fitting, that there is an ordained way of doing things which must not be put at risk by individualistic feelings:

> *But you must know your father lost a father,*
> *That father lost, lost his, and the survivor bound*
> *In filial obligation for some term*
> *To do obsequious sorrow. (2, 2, 89-)*

Hamlet replies that the forms of grief, the rites that attend death, do not matter. What matters is "that within", personal feeling. Already, in this important scene, two different ways of looking at the world, one which argues in terms of precedent and tradition - an essentially feudal view - and the other who argues in terms of personal feeling - an essentially post-feudal view - are being argued out. And, crucially, the medium for that argument is death and what it means. We see from this early scene, which comes even before Hamlet's encounter with the Ghost, that death is to be the battleground for Hamlet's individuality.

8. If the play is about death, where does all the stuff about theatre and players come into it?

Hamlet, as we know from his long and detailed advice to the Players and the delight he takes in the whole idea of the play-within-a-play, fancies himself as a stage-manager. And what he seeks to do throughout the play is to stage-manage death, to make it as significant as a work of theatre that has been rehearsed, that is performed at the right time and in the right way.

It is interesting, for instance, that although Old Hamlet commands his son to "Remember me" and Hamlet promises to do so, yet he remembers almost nothing of his living father. His conjuring of his father for Gertrude (3, 4, 54-) is a formal eulogy, a conscious performance made with a deliberate eye to its effect. But it is in marked contrast even to the warmth of his memories of his father's jester Yorick. There is no touching, intimate scene in his memory of his father. What he keeps in mind, what he mulls over, what obsesses him is the manner of his father's death, its details and its timing, the fact that it was unrehearsed:

A took my father grossly, full of bread,
With all his crimes broad blown, as flush as May;
And how his audit stands, who knows save heaven?
(3, 3, 80-)

And so he literally rehearses it, instructs his actors, has it acted out. He tries to give to death, which throughout the play is sudden and messy, the form and order of a work of art. He becomes an aesthete of death from the moment he begins to ponder his task, just as later he will be careful about specifying the manner and timing of death even for the hapless and insignificant Rosencrantz and Guildenstern : "not shriving time allowed".

This is the significance of the "To be or not to be" soliloquy (3, 1, 56) and its contemplation of suicide. He talks of suicide like a connoisseur judging a good painting. He wants to know, not if it is morally justified, or useful, or pleasant, but whether it is "nobler in the mind", whether it is lofty and well-shaped. He talks of death as a "consummation", something that is honed and finished and achieved. This is the significance also of Hamlet's refusal to kill Claudius in Act 3, scene 3. This scene is generally taken as proof of the fact that Hamlet is guilty of improper delay, that he is unable to make his mind up to do what he ought to. His reasoning that Claudius is praying and therefore would go to heaven if he killed is taken as an excuse and a very lame one. But in fact it is absolutely in keeping with the way Hamlet thinks about death throughout the play.

What he wants for Claudius' death is a kind of symmetry, an artistic harmony matching his own father's death. Old Hamlet died without having time to confess his sins; so must Claudius die. What Hamlet has done is to convince himself that he can use his own reasoning, his education in philosophy and the theatre to make the death which he has to perform something orderly and fitting rather than something savage and belonging to the visceral irrational world of mere revenge. The death of Old Hamlet at one end of the scale will be balanced by the death in the same circumstances of Claudius at the other end. Something bloody, vicious, and dark will be made to look like something shaped, balanced, proper. The things that are not dreamt of in Horatio's philosophy will at least be managed according to that philosophy.

9.   Where does the Ghost come into it?

For Hamlet, then, the idea of death and the idea of theatre become strangely inter-related. And they are related right from the moment when the ghost lays the burden of revenge on Hamlet. The very first thing Hamlet does after his encounter with the ghost is to enter into an elaborate and highly theatrical ceremony of swearing, a ceremony that he takes such great delight in that he keeps repeating it, somewhat to the puzzlement of Horatio and Marcellus. The idea of the ceremony strikes him suddenly and forcefully. He says that "without more circumstance (i.e. ceremony) at all,/I hold it fit that we shake hands and part", and then a few seconds later begins to insist on his elaborate ceremonials. And it is at this moment, that Shakespeare chooses one of the oddest devices of the play, a device that is there specifically to remind us of the theatre itself, to remind us that we are watching a performance of a play. When Marcellus objects to Hamlet's insistence that they swear again on his sword not to reveal the happenings of the night to anyone, the Ghost cries out "Swear" from under the stage. His voice reminds us that there is an actor who has gone through a trap-door under the stage, that this is a play and we have just seen a theatrical trick - the disappearance of the ghost.

And in case we miss the point, Hamlet makes a joke to draw it to our attention. Hamlet has just had an awesome encounter with a terrifying ghost, the ghost of his father whom he holds in the highest respect. But what he says when he hears the "Swear" coming from under the stage is "Ha, ha, boy, sayest thou so? Art thou there, truepenny?"/Come on. You hear this fellow in the cellarage./ Consent to swear." "Boy", "truepenny", "this fellow in the cellarage" - these are not the terms an awe-struck son uses about the ghost of his dead father. They are the terms an actor uses about one of his colleagues. The actor playing Hamlet says "Come on, you hear this old so-and-so under the floorboards, let's get on with it." It is a joke, the kind of joke that Shakespeare often injects immediately after a scene of great solemnity and tension, but it is one which serves to remind us that the ghost we have just seen is a trick, that we are watching three actors, that this, in a sense, is a play about performance, that Hamlet is trying to stage-manage something. The connection which Hamlet makes between theatricality and the manner of death is not something which happens only in the scenes with the Players in the second act, but something which is planted in his mind at the very moment that he takes on his task of killing Claudius.

10. If Hamlet is a stage-manager, is he a good one?

The effectiveness of theatricality in actually shaping or coping with reality is always ambivalent in the play. Hamlet's "O, what a rogue and peasant slave am I!" soliloquy throws strong doubt on the relationship between theatricality and reality: the actor can put on a show of emotion and "all for nothing". Hamlet, though, chooses to ignore his own doubts and by the end of the same speech (2, 2, 533-) has convinced himself that theatre can reveal the truth, that "The play's the thing/Wherein I'll catch the conscience of the king."

What Hamlet believes he can stage-manage, what he is most concerned with, is boundaries. He is concerned with the boundary between life and death, between this life and the next. He focuses constantly on the moment of death and how it affects the passage into the next life.

He thinks about this moment, this boundary line, in relation to four separate deaths - his father's, Claudius', Rosencrantz and Guildenstern's and his own. He believes that he can fix that line, choose the right moment of death that will determine what will happen after death. His father was killed without confession and Hamlet fears that he may be damned. Claudius he will not kill while he may be in a state of grace. Rosencrantz and Guildenstern, he specifies in his forged letter, must be killed without allowing time for confession of their sins. As for himself, he rejects suicide in the "To be or not to be" speech precisely because it would not allow him to determine the passage he will make into death. In suicide, the afterlife would be unknown, unpredictable, "The undiscovered country, from whose bourn no traveller returns..." The reason why

Hamlet, by the fifth act, is prepared to face his end, is that he believes that he knows the boundary, that the passage will be significant, providential, artistically shaped. He can tell Horatio that "There is a special providence in the fall of a sparrow. If it be now, 'tis not to come; if be not to come, it will be now; if it be not now, yet it will come. The readiness is all." (5, 2, 208) He is ready for his death, he has rehearsed it, it will be all right on the night.

11.   And is it all right?

Hamlet's tragedy is that he is wrong about his ability to fix the boundaries of life and death. He says that death is a country from which "no traveller returns" but he should know that this is not so, for he has already seen his father return from death. Throughout the play, the categories of life and death refuse to hold. They seep into each other, constantly blur their boundaries, so that Hamlet's belief that the boundary can be fixed and achieved becomes impossible. Right from the start of the play, the rites by which we separate life from death, the rituals of funeral and burial, have been disrupted, are failing to function properly. Claudius' first speech (1, 2) is about the way in which the rituals of life (marriage) and those of death (funeral) have been mixed up and his language mirrors the uncomfortable contradiction, yoking together opposites in an uneasy alliance:

...as twere with a defeated joy,
With an auspicious and a dropping eye
With mirth in funeral and with dirge in marriage,...

And, as the play goes on, those rites break down completely. The dead Polonius, in the fourth act, is denied his proper funeral ("we have done but greenly", says Claudius "in hugger-mugger to inter him"). The dead Ophelia in the fifth act is given the truncated funeral rites that cause Laertes to ask repeatedly "What ceremony else?"'

We should profane the service of the dead
To sing a requiem and such rest to her
As to peace-parted souls.   (5, 1, 224-)

And finally the graveyard itself is desecrated by Hamlet and Laertes fighting in it, trying to kill each other in an open grave, the ultimate symbol of burial without the proper rituals. The public rites which mark the passage between life and death have collapsed completely.

But it is not just the rituals marking the boundaries of life and death which refuse to hold. In the very imaginations of the characters, the distinction between the two keeps getting blurred. Hamlet himself can hardly think of a dead person without imagining them alive. When he has just killed Polonius he imagines him as he was when he was alive and proceeds to talk to him in exactly the same sarcastic way we have seen him use earlier:

Indeed, this counsellor
Is now most still, most secret, and most grave,
Who was in life a foolish prating knave.
Come, sir, to draw toward an end with you. (3, 4, 214-)

The very pun on "grave" sums up the blurring of life and death, for it is both an attribute of a living person and a symbol of death. Hamlet is always resurrecting the dead. His father is re-born in his son's eulogies of him. He resurrects the dead Ophelia as an object of love after he has spurned the living woman. And, of course, in the scene with Yorick's skull, he brings his father's dead jester back to life.

12.   What about the skull?

This, indeed, is the point of the Yorick scene (5, 1, 167-). There is probably no scene in any play ever written that has become so much of a cliche and that has suffered so much as a consequence. Hamlet, looking at the skull, is not staring into the emptiness of death. Rather he is filling that emptiness, bringing it back to life, re-creating Yorick with a warmth and humanity that are in marked contrast to the beautiful but lifeless eulogy of his own dead father. In this speech, the living and the dead mingle with a startling intimacy. The dead man's skull had lips that Hamlet kissed. He played tricks, gave piggyback rides. He sang, tumbled, told jokes. What we get is not a speech about the futility of life, but a speech about the wonder of life, about how much is lost in death. Looking at a rotten and smelly skull, Hamlet can give us a sense of the sadness of death which he and the court of Elsinore cannot manage for any of the real deaths which take place within the play.

Here, the borders of life and death have been completely broken. Just as at the start of the play Claudius remembers the mixture of wedding and funeral, so here Hamlet creates a sense of madcap fun in a graveyard, invoking a feast that reminds us of the earlier wedding feast ("your flashes of merriment that were wont to set the table on a roar"). The Gravedigger adds to the scene's blurring of the distinction between life and death: when Hamlet asks him how long it will take a man to rot in the grave, the Gravedigger immediately thinks of living people who are already like dead ones: "if 'a be not rotten before 'a die", and goes on to conjure up the image of a living man, a tanner, at his trade. He then talks of water decaying dead bodies, which reminds us immediately of a live body - Ophelia - that we have just heard of being decayed and destroyed by water. All the time in the scene the distinction between the living and the dead is being broken down. And this, too is the cause of Hamlet's pain. For in looking at death and invoking life, Hamlet invokes sex.

13. But there's no sex in Hamlet, surely?

Throughout the play sex is the essence of life, but as life becomes mixed up with death, so sex becomes mixed up with death. Even before he meets the ghost, Hamlet's torment has come from the mixture of sex and death - his father's death and his mother's wedding. Looking at Yorick's skull, he cannot help but think of a woman in her bedroom: "Now get you to my lady's chamber, and tell her, let her paint an inch thick, to this favour she must come."

And this is true throughout the play. In one of the play's most shocking images, the "mad" Hamlet, talking to Polonius, mixes sexual generation with death, and both with Ophelia: "if the sun breed maggots in a dead dog, being a good kissing carrion -Have you a daughter?" (2, 2, 181-) Death becomes birth and the whole is mixed up with his own desire for Ophelia. And in the play's imagery, maggots themselves, the life that is being born from the dead dog, are connected back to death : "We fat ourselves for maggots". (4, 3, 22)

72

Sex and death become enmeshed even in the flowers that Ophelia is carrying in her own mad scene. Gertrude talks of the "long purples", flowers that "liberal shepherds give a grosser name/But our cold maids do dead men's fingers call them." (4, 7, 169-) The same flower, in the shepherds' rude name, can be associated with sex, or it can, in the name the maids give it, be associated with dead bodies.

14. Maybe the Freudians were right, and Hamlet needs a good psychoanalyst?

It is important to remember that this confusion of sex and death is not primarily psychological. It does not come about because Hamlet wants to sleep with his mother, or with a dead dog, or even with a maggot. It comes from the blurring of distinctions, of rigid categories which is rooted in the play's place at a point of transition between one world view and another. We are not shown it as something internal, something happening in Hamlet's soul or subconscious. We are shown it is as something public, something that is connected to the breakdown of institutions and indeed of the entire state of Denmark. For just as the public rituals which separate life from death - the funerals and burials - break down in the course of the play, so too do the public institutions that contain sexual life - the family, the very distinction between men and women.

What happens to Ophelia when her father dies and she goes mad is that she begins to confuse her father with her would-be lover, Hamlet. A dead man is confused with a living man and that confusion of life and death becomes a confusion of sexual and familial roles. Her song of mourning (4, 5, 23) is for her "true love", who is "dead and gone", but, of course, it is not her true love (Hamlet) who is dead, but her father. And she also confuses men and women. When she is leaving, she says "sweet ladies, good night, good night", though two of the three people she is talking to are men. And when she returns later in the scene, she again confuses father and lover in her song, this time more explicitly: "It is the false steward that stole his master's daughter". In reality, her grief concerns the false master (Hamlet) that did not steal his steward's daughter (Ophelia). Laertes understands that there is meaning in this seeming distraction: "This nothing's more than matter." (4, 5, 171)

15. Where does a nice girl like Ophelia get such thoughts from?

In all of this, Ophelia is only following Hamlet himself, and in particular what Hamlet has done to her. The mocking Hamlet, horrified by the confusion of sexual roles implicit in his mother marrying her husband's brother, takes up this confusion of sexual roles and sexual identity. On leaving for England he calls to Claudius "Farewell, dear mother." When Claudius corrects him, he enjoys himself with the way in which, in Elsinore, sexual categories have ceased to hold together: "My mother - father and mother is man and wife, man and wife is one flesh, and so, my mother."(4, 3, 50-) But this confusion of sexual categories is far from funny in what he has already done to Ophelia. Ophelia, in her "mad" confusion of father and lover, is only repeating Hamlet's confusion of mother and lover in his cruel attack on her fragile identity. Hamlet's baiting of Ophelia in Act 3, scene 1, comes shortly before his confrontation with his mother in Act 3, scene 4 and it is a rehearsal for that confrontation. It is Hamlet being the stage-manager, trying out the power of his words to turn into daggers. What he accuses Ophelia of - lustfulness and sexual inconstancy - is what he wants to accuse his mother of. He uses her as a substitute for his mother, deprives her of her proper category. And something deprived of its proper category, of its place in the catalogue, can easily get lost. This is what happens to Ophelia.

Shakespeare has shown us an Ophelia who is shaped and formed and defined by others, in particular by men. She is defined in turn by Laertes, Polonius, and Hamlet and deserted in turn by each. She has no identity of her own, only that which is constructed for her by others. In Act 1, scene 3, she replies to Polonius' question as to what she should think with "I do not know, my lord, what I should think." Subsequently she replies to Hamlet's similar question as to her thoughts: "I think nothing, my lord." All her actions and responses are about what other people think for her and of her before they disappear and her defining forces are removed.

Ophelia is the play's image of what happens when things and people become undefined, when set categories refuse to hold their place. The problem for Hamlet is that even while the distinction between life and death is falling apart in the most intimate of ways throughout the play, he still maintains the belief that he can manipulate that distinction, that he can pinpoint the boundary between life and death and use it to his own ends. In this he is terribly wrong. The action of the play itself, as it gathers force, makes this abundantly clear to us. Hamlet says that he will "defy augury" but this is untrue because there is a building pattern of prophecy in the play which turns out to be true.

16.   Where does prophecy come into it?

The play has premonitions of death, areas in which the distinction between life and death breaks down to such a degree that the living already appear to be dead. Ophelia mourns her dead lover (Hamlet) while Hamlet is still alive. Hamlet talks of dead kings - Alexander, Caesar - and then says "Here comes the king" (5, 1, 204) meaning Claudius, prefiguring the death of the living Claudius by associating him with the dead. And, most starkly, both Hamlet and Laertes, who are to die together, jump into the same open grave. Hamlet's belief that life and death will keep their places is being contradicted throughout the final acts by what we see and hear.

17.   Well, at least there's no politics.

There is. What motivates Hamlet throughout the play is his belief that death can be made orderly, can be made rational, can, in fact become a solution. And he sees it as a solution not just to his own troubles, but to the troubles and injustices of the wider world. The "To be or not to be" speech in which he considers the benefits of suicide, far from being the speech of an isolated neurotic, is the speech of a man with a keen political sense and a sharp social knowledge. Its imagery is full of the reality of a corrupt world - oppression, the arrogance of the powerful, the malfunctioning of the law. To its images of injustice are added images of hard labour, of grunting and sweating under heavy loads. It is an extraordinary speech to come from a prince of the realm, a full and terrible picture of social inequality. Clearly, that inequality and injustice weigh on Hamlet, and we know from what Claudius says that Hamlet is popular with the mob, with the same people who come to the door with Laertes looking for the world to be made new.

And it is precisely as a vehicle for equality that Hamlet is attracted to death. On the one hand, by matching Claudius' death with that of Old Hamlet, he can make things equal in that respect. And on the other hand, he views death as a more general leveller, as that which makes social divisions equal. "Your fat king and your lean beggar is but variable service - two dishes, but to one table." Or, "a king may go a progress through the guts of a beggar." (4, 3, 23-)

And in one of the more complicated set of images in the play, he brings these two senses of equality together - his own struggle with Claudius and the general equalisation of social distinctions. He uses images of fishing in Act 4, scene 2 and in Act 5, scene 1, comparing himself to a fish and Claudius to an angler ("Thrown out his angle for my proper life"), and he also sees the man fishing with a worm which has eaten the dead body of a king as the ultimate proof of human equality: "A man may fish with the worm that hath eat of a king and eat of the fish that hath fed of that worm." Far from contemplating death as mere non-existence, Shakespeare has Hamlet draw on the powerful radical tradition of using death - "Death the Leveller" - as an image for the dissolution of social classes. Death, the very thing which Hamlet believes can define boundaries in the play, can bring order and shape to things that have gone awry, is also being used as an image of the breaking of boundaries. In this double-action is the real tragedy of *Hamlet*.

18.   Why is the ending such a mess of corpses?

The thing about Hamlet's attempts to stage-manage a death that will be orderly, well-formed, and, above all, meaningful is that it goes horribly wrong, is mocked at every turn by the action of the play and in particular by Hamlet's own actions. He kills Polonius by mistake, in a sordid, meaningless way and ends up having to "lug the guts into the neighbour room" (3, 4, 213) and hide the body without ceremony, without justice, without any sense of rightness or balance. This is why his reaction on discovering that the person he has killed is Polonius and not Claudius is one, not of horror, sorrow or remorse, as we might expect, but one of anger. He immediately begins to berate the corpse, like a director berating an actor who has wandered on in the wrong scene and spoiled his effects. And again, when his actions lead to the death of Ophelia, his reaction to her funeral in the graveyard is a petulant one, that of an actor who has ben upstaged, demanding his rightful place in the action over lesser actors like Laertes.

His last throw of the dice is on his own death. The scene in which Hamlet, Laertes, Gertrude and Claudius die is in itself almost a play-within-a-play. It is a formal show organised before a court audience, with all the ceremonies that should attach to such a formal performance. It harks back both to the scene with the Players and to the earlier elaborate ceremony of swearing over Hamlet's sword. It is pure theatre, with all the appropriate props - the poisoned cup and the poisoned sword, the trumpet blasts, even the applause of an appreciative crowd - of a big theatrical death scene. But far from being inevitable, far from us having the sense of a fated event working its way out, it is a shambles. It is a mess. It is all about "purposes mistook fall'n on th'inventors heads". Hamlet cannot even kill Claudius cleanly and singly. He has to, as it were, kill him twice, with poison and with stabbing. The single act which should balance out everything becomes double. Nothing will work out as it should, nothing will stick to its place in the script.

And even then, what is on Hamlet's mind? He wants his story to be told, he wants his life and death to be given the shape and significance of a work of art: "And in this harsh world draw thy breath in pain, To tell my story." He still believes that his death, in the midst of all of these "casual slaughters" can be individual, can have significance and shape.

He dies. The play is over. Hamlet will be remembered. He will have given to at least one death in this succession of deaths a meaning. Horatio speaks a loving and lovely lullaby: "Good night, sweet prince,/And flights of angels sing thee to thy rest."

But the play is not over. Drums beat. An Ambassador enters, someone we have not seen before in the play. What does he have to say? "That Rosencrantz and Guildenstern are dead." He comes to announce, at the moment when Hamlet seems to have at last given to death some significance, a completely insignificant set of deaths, completely without meaning, something wandering in from another part of the play, a couple of minor players staggering onstage at the climax to upstage the star. The play itself should be over but refuses to close. Even with his death, Hamlet has achieved nothing. We are in a truly tragic world, left with only the straw man, the man who will die for a straw and is puffed up with ambition, who will countenance "The imminent death of twenty thousand men" for the sake of "a fantasy and trick of fame". Fortinbras, the man who sends thousands to their slaughter for no good reason, is hardly someone to make a single, individual death meaningful. He is the ultimate image of Hamlet's failure.